THE WHITE BROTHER

THE COLLECTED WRITINGS OF
MICHAEL JUSTE

IN TWO VOLUMES
VOLUME 1

TITLES IN THIS SERIES

THE WHITE BROTHER

An Occult Autobiography

Michael Juste

THE WILD GANDER PRESS
MINNEAPOLIS—ST. PAUL

First published 1927.

ISBN 978-1-956796-10-0 (hardback); 978-1-956796-06-3 (paperback).

https://www.thewildgander.press

CONTENTS

DEDICATION

Dedicated to "THE BROTHERS."

NOTE ON THE TEXT

The White Brother was first published in 1927 by Rider and Co. of London. Until now, it has never been reprinted. A small number of misprints and errors have been silently emended; citations have been updated and a bibliography added; and the many quotations from M., originally run in, are now set in block style. Otherwise the text remains unchanged.

Part One

PREFACE

Seeking in the box of talents hidden in the lumber-room of my mind, the only gift my ancestors left me, for their material substance had vanished long ago, I found, among a strange assortment of old, rusty and broken gifts, a clean and brightly coloured quill pen. Over this I pondered. "With what mental nourishment," I mused, "can I feed it? My shoes have not gathered the dust of the roads, nor have I wandered to tropical or icy lands, where stalwart and steely-eyed Adventure awaits the traveller. Nor have I dined upon the intellectual and leathery food of academic learning. Then to what use can I put this newly found instrument?"

Murmured a quiet voice, "Your mental journeyings, have you forgotten them? If you will write of your mental and occult adventures, I will also give to you some new teachings that I think will interest the mystical and Theosophic student."

So accepting my teacher's offer, for I am a pupil to one who has woven into my thought the finely spun fabric of lofty, but not impossible, ideals, and who has been as a bridge for me between two worlds, this dwarfish sphere and the ever-increasing loveliness of the spirit, I accepted with great joy his offer, and write that which I hope minds and hearts will welcome.

For this is the chronicle of a student who sought and became the pupil of one deeply learned in the knowledge of the Divine Sciences. And it has been written as a record and in the hope that those who read will know that upon this planet dwell brothers who are willing and *eager* to help those who seek a knowledge of divine things.

THE WANDERERS OF JUPITER

Greetings from the immortals of the hills to those of the valleys! To those who are sleeping, to those who have slept and have now awakened! All twisted words will be straightened before the nuptials of Truth. Silken flatteries will be exchanged for honest linen, and the white robes worn by all.

Greetings to the wanderers, for homes will be given them. The sun will awaken in their hearts and its rays flame from their foreheads, and the rays will flash from their hands like swords of fire to those who have measured falsely. For the wanderers will be the servants of Jupiter, who will again awaken.

Greetings and love from the hidden brothers to all!

INCARNATION: A DREAM

It was time to dive into the wilderness of matter; to don the suit of flesh and to gather the material of the soul, the harvested vices and virtues of past lives; to leave shining regions where love flowered simply and sweetly beyond the thralldom of Time. A realm where beings unhurried and unperturbed created, by calm thought, the birth of events for the guidance and growth of the voyager named Man.

The chart of my journey lay before me. Dark rocks, veiled in the manes of charging seas, shone sombrely on the animated map of my future life. Stark headlands, smooth and rising high, and glowing as though plated in sheets of bronze, helmeted with bare, razor-sharpened stones, stood sternly amid the angry waves, wherein the reflection of a small cloud-blurred sun grimaced, distorted by the ripples; while the twin tides of darkness and day ebbed and flowed with a horrible monotony about that strangely bearded world.

The crude stone nests of man lay huddled in vast, shapeless masses, beaded with innumerable spots of light that dawned at night and set at morn, and I seemed to hear faint threads of sound, heavy with anguish and sorrow, ascend from this globe and plaintively and slowly die away, mingled with the sighs of irregular breathing, that rose from parched souls that slept through the hovering tides of night. And white-coned humps and tree-burdened carapaces that grew upon this dark and terrible planet, passed in slow procession before my eyes. Only the glimmering ribbon of river and stream and the humble scent of shy flowers gave me a little strength for my coming journey.

And, as I watched the vision of my preordained pilgrimage, a gentle voice murmured to me: "In that small sphere dwell the wild-souled ones, whose agonized frames are scorched by the fires of burning and ravenous hearts. There, destructive and wilful gods dwell, the brethren and musicians who play to their inhabitants malignant rhapsodies, evoking from them a terrible choir of pain. Peer more deeply into the veilings of that picture."

Shudderingly and fearfully, I obeyed, and the chart of my voyage dissolved before the shrinking eyes of the spirit; for a shadowy arena rose, wherein filmy clouds of scarlet and grey mist swirled and writhed like living fumes amid convulsed and frenzied throngs, who shrieked and grappled and fought with one another. Above the circle titanic and evil gods upon their thrones, a terrible concourse of the dark passions and powers, whose eyes, fiery with a vast lust, glared piercingly upon the tormented; yet these gods were the monstrous children of the battling hosts, created from the fierce hates and desires of mankind through the ages.

Here sat gaunt and thin-fleshed Hunger, naked, bowed and swaying, a sickly flame wavering feebly in his eyes, for he could gain no nourishment from his makers, but only the pangs of starvation. And nearby crouched the crooning and mumbling hag, Madness, her sparse and grey dishevelled hair entangled in torn garments that showed a yellow and withered flesh, while her long fingers scrabbled and tore desperately at spectres her glazed and shining eyes alone could see, and a watery foam trickled from her loosely hanging lips. I saw the god of War, with the head of a wolf and a mane that curtained him in a deep red fire, howling a song of evil joy.

Jealousy and Hate, Lust and Greed, all sat gazing into the circle, and hungrily banqueted upon the pains of the tormented; their jaws, lit by gleaming tusks, opening wide and rolling forth a hideous antiphony, a rhythmic laughter, a black and unholy merriment, wherein trembled deep notes of weeping, rising from the strangling souls, and dwindling away into a bleak and distant harmony. It was a deadly laughter that shook the frame of that small world, re-echoing in my soul till the dark flame of sound enfolded my senses like a burning shroud, until I could bear the vision and pain no longer, but turned away and watched in the distance the gathering of the swift and slim oreads upon the green and blossom-sprinkled mountain summits. I saw their hair like veils of snowy mist; their pale and flower-like faces aureoled in an imperceptible nimbus; their illusive limbs dancing in harmony to the vague tremor of the redolent winds that fluttered and caressed their cerements, as nebulous as their forms, that constantly dissolved and reappeared from the viewless elements of the air. And a wavering and thinly spun web of music drifted languidly up from the faun-haunted valleys, where the tree tops, whose boughs and leaves shone like delicate and crystalline green flames, quivered and swayed in the hyaline air, while brushed by the filmy garments of the never-resting sylphs. While from a nearby pool of unruffled and clear, golden water, a gentle fair-tressed nymph rose smoothly and sorrowfully to bid me farewell. From this realm of serene youth, of white and flower-wreathed temples—here gods, child-like and simple, the essence of unforgotten and eternal wisdom, were worshipped—was I banished, to dive and drown in the malicious and turbulent waves of passion and desire!

Slowly the nebulous oreads grew more vague, their light and illusive strains of song lingering and echoing into my muffled senses, becoming finer and finer, waning away upon heights my weakening hearing could no longer follow. The serene mountain crests loomed from an ever-increasing distance; the white temples became blurred and wore a mask of deepening grey that spread before my eyes; while a diaphanous mist, trembling amid the shining woodlands, gradually hid from my sight the nymphs and fauns whose fragile music had long since ebbed, leaving me poised within an abyss of deathly and utter stillness. And in that great pause, love and peace, and all the quiet moods and visions of the spirit, were erased, ere I was drawn into the conflict of matter.

Desperately and in terrible anguish I struggled, for an invisible current drew me helplessly along, gasping and shuddering against the coarse contact of the world of matter that wrapped me in a black mass of suffocating force. I sank, with a host of other weeping spirits, into the prison-house of clay, and with a last cry of agony, became unconscious.

MERLIN AWAKE!

Merlin awake! and with your magic enchant the woods and waters. Strike our eyelids with your wand, that we may see the moonlight-loving nymph; the sea-robed nereid and the cloud-veiled sylph; the salamander in the core of flame, and the bearded gnome enshrined in the breast of Earth. Call again the troubadours from their heavy slumber to serenade the evening lily at her casement. Trumpet to the tournament the knights of chivalry, encased in their glinting petals of silver and gold. Bid them raise their pennons in the grey mist of today.

*   *   *   *   *

Ere the clay can be refined to feel the sweet wind of the spirit and hear the faint whisper of the wisdom that moves the stars; ere the soul can sense the harmonious rhythm in the most sombre and chaotic of things, and walk beneath the calm splendour of timeless morn—it must be clad in the dark vestments of sorrow. The vault of day must fade into starless night, blurring the hills where the heralds of beauty trumpet forth their messages to man.

Souls that would be prometheans, must conquer the dragon within, and the mirage that would allure them from the white road. The strength of impassive cliffs and the delicate swiftness of the hind will be theirs, when they have conquered. But before victory comes the loneliness of the night.

If they are the reed-blowers who re-echo the music of Nature, the reeds will become brittle and cracked, and chords once clearly heard will be faint as remembered fragrance. The instrument and the canvas, the hammer and the machine will be laid aside. For all things will be sapless and without nourishment. The winged steeds of the imagination shall sleep, but from the seeds of torment will grow the flowers of amaranth.

CHAPTER ONE
A GREY SPRING

I came to birth in a sallow and bedraggled quarter of a great city, where servile and lean-faced beings lounged through narrow, malodorous courts, and sickly, colourless streets, their lips spitting lecherous words, their eyes burning with hunger, or leering with lust.

In this grey atmosphere, among thousands more, was I born. A wanderer burdened with the cross of poverty. What terrible sin we weak-limbed souls had committed, I know not. Nevertheless, my position was not as bad as the position of many others, for my parents were not illiterate, coarse, or unclean; they were simply poor, and they possessed a strong moral fibre that was as a prop to their children, giving them strength to combat the twisted desires and passions that moulded the souls of many made weak through great sufferings and starved character.

Our world was painted in all the tints of grey; grey streets, grey faces, grey minds and hearts. It was as though they had been wrought and sketched, when in the last phases of cynicism, by an embittered and unsuccessful painter. And the attitudes and drabness of these poor people's lives seemed to be the result of his philosophy of despair. The voices that hurt the air were loud and unmusical; language was battered and monotonously livid with oaths; laughter was harsh and jeering, and as laughter shows the imprint and state of the soul, so one could read within those ragged voices the symbols of thoughtless and unhampered desires. One could say that they had characters that had never been given a wash; characters whereon the soot of the city lay thickly spread.

Now the people suffered from a soul-disease. If they had had any physical plague the Medical Authorities would have had them taken away, and their houses cleansed and disinfected, but as they only suffered from mental and moral sicknesses, that were equally catching, they were permitted to spread these diseases to their numerous, unclean offspring. And now I see them from a different standpoint. I see them all as children who had run away from their great and kind mother Nature. Becoming as lost children, neglected and made vicious, cunning and mindless in the whirlpool of a great, cold, and uninterested city.

Here savagery had truly become the stepmother, and had usurped the throne of humanity's true parent: Nature, vaccinating her helpless stepchildren with her own evil virus, that bleared the bright eye and made bloodless the fresh and fair skin of youth.

It was society in an unshaven state, whose unwashed and uncombed atmosphere muddied and blotted out the nobler spots of the soul. And such was its power, that only the unconquerable and finer spirit of a man could emerge. But it was not poverty alone that discoloured and begrimed these forlorn streets, but something more terrible, more potent for evil and pain; it was ignorance. It was this appalling ignorance that made poverty so horrible, so beastly. Made the gaiety, language and manners of these people one long, continuous nightmare.

Had these people even a sense of beauty, the streets and rooms in which they dwelt would have become more bearable, and less like a conception of a fifth-rate Hades. And how arrogant they were! How snobbish! How wasteful! What pictures arise in my mind as I think of them all.

I see an old, stunted woman, like an animated witch's cauldron wherein stirs all the venom gathered from the jungle undergrowth of slumland, standing, with raggedly clothed body, rage-contorted and vigorous with hate beneath the sweating and rumbling darkness of a railway arch. Her thin hands, black-rimmed and wrinkled, old and blotched and loose-skinned, beneath which run hot currents of gin-poisoned blood are raised threateningly against the sky, as though cursing it. She seems to be the ultimate essences of all the virtues of Hell, and standing before a group of amused spectators, a foul thing invisibly framed in a medley of stale and throat-suffocating smells, her cackling and twisted voice croaks its drunken song of blasphemy.

Here is Saturday night, and men and women, upon whom the finery of another day was mellowed, shuffle and sprawl, and hiccough unmelodiously, sentimental songs to a double moon, or into one another's bleared and misty faces. The crash of breaking glass, and the curse and shriek of a woman mingled with the low growls of a man, startles the ear.

It is Saturday night, and there is a feverish quality in the air. Previous to dusk, a thin, clinging rain has endeavoured to refresh a somewhat clamorous, hectic day. But only for a little while did it drop, then ceased in a vague, forlorn manner. And now the pavements and roadways have taken advantage of the moisture, and mingle the dust and the rain in a film of sticky, grey mud. A mud that seems natural and fitting for the monotonous streets and grimy, bruised-looking houses. A mud that is a fitting symbol to the muddiness of the people's lives and thoughts. A mud that would cake later on into blobs of dust about the lower clothing of the inhabitants. And now, the slums having been garbed in their natural hues, the flaring, blaring night sets in.

The plain street lamps hesitate, then spring into light at the touch of the shabby lamplighters, illuminating, in a blurred manner, the damp, stale-smelling streets wherefrom move mingled anxiety and savagery in the forms of men and women, marketwards. Let there be no false sentiment. For there were few unused and full of anguish at the manner in which they lived. For imagination, lofty ambition and restlessness at the state in which they lived were known and felt by few. Victory in a quarrel; windfalls in a gamble; and a lengthy public-house debauch were the golden moments of their lives. Though often black periods of imprisonment occurred, these were accepted philosophically.

Towards the yellow and red, green and purple masses of fruit and vegetables, crowned with jets of hissing fire, and stalls asprawl with clumsy cabbages, recklessly piled mounds of potatoes, and other produce, these people move. The air warm and filled with the clamour of hoarsely bellowing voices; loudly bargaining voices; soft, gentlemanly voices of quacks; and plaintive voices of pedlars and beggars. While children make cunning attempts to steal from unwatchful costers.

It is Saturday night, and unconscious comedy, impulsive brutality, and harrowing tragedy are quickened in their movements. And oh, the loudness of their voices; the never-ending loudness of their voices.

Once we lived in a court. I was very young then, but I still remember the picture of a woman who had run away from a fight. She had also broken a pane of glass and her hands were smothered in blood that she washed away beneath the tap in our yard. I believe she was a notorious, drunken character, and she lived in the disreputable quarter of the court —our part was respectable—singing and shouting and quarrelling night after night. I gazed in wonder at her agitated appearance, at her torn dress and blouse, and flushed face. There was no attempt on the part of the group that surrounded her to send the children away. We were supposed to be used to such things. But we did not live long in that place.

In these streets, children, with delightful naïveté, indulged in the full-fledged sins of maturity. And even now I can hear the continual whimpering and shouting of these children. Sharp-faced and neglected ones whose mouths re-echoed the foul oaths of their elders; and the more foul, the prouder became their parents. And though the sun shone as brightly in our quarter as elsewhere, yet mentally, I have always seen those streets draped in a veil of perpetual twilight and mist. It was an atmosphere that, like a hidden cowl, oppressed and depressed all those living within its orbit. A district wherein stunted and bleak houses, painted by dirt and time, with mouldering brickwork, battered doors and trembling staircases, with windows holding tattered wisps of curtain or oblongs of cardboard and stuffed sacks, stood or leaned in abject or forlorn rows, while upon greasy steps sat groups of slatternly women and their dirty offspring. Squalor spread a thick film over all, and for a sensitive and imaginative child it was a heavy and continual horror.

And now, as remembrance unrolls before me this sad tapestry of the past, I see this city in its true spirit. She is a handsome-headed and richly crowned queen; with passionate, shining eyes and diamond-glittering teeth; with wide-open, laughing lips and berouged cheeks; wearing a collar of sparkling gold and a long patched and tattered gown of grey that is thickly encrusted with the mud and grime that lies heavily over so many parts of her domain. A motionless stately queen, whose laughter, deep and merry, drowns the discordancy evoked from fiercely stabbing despair. But the mirror of her eyes cannot mask the truth, for they reflect to me the dreams of her myriad subjects: dreams flowering up from the glowing and bright furnaces of youth, and blown down like withered leaves; dreams of a rare and delicate substance born from the hearts of newly awakened lovers; all, all to be shrivelled and scattered by the icy winds of mature cynicism. Weak and feverish dreams born from the sapless minds of old age; dreams of thin, large-eyed children whose little wishes could not be born; pale and wan, passionate and lustful, tender and frail; an endless flood of dreams, like a mist of rainbows rushing upwards behind the windows of her eyes and vanishing, rarely to return. While to her ears surge great waves of voices from the ocean of sound: turbulent and placid, rapid and lingering, loudly and drowsily, beating into her mind their burning loves and hates. A great stony-hearted spirit and queen marred and made imperfect through the imperfection of her subjects.

In this city, till the age of fourteen, my mind was fed upon a feeble and watery diet misnamed Education, that was decorated and coloured by the rich, indigestible foods of royal history. But royal history is the caviar of national incident, and like caviar should be given in small quantities. And these mental luxuries were given to children, who really could not appreciate them. We were regaled upon the exploits of the Elizabethan buccaneers; upon the immense growth of the Empire; upon the conquest of the inferior and humbler races of the world by the power of sword and gun of the lordly white man. Oh, yes, we were also taught the Ten Commandments, such as: "Thou Shalt Not Steal," and the rest.

In these large and comfortless rooms the importance of knowing the names of the rivers in Africa and the animals of India, and something about the habits of the peoples of the various continents, were strongly emphasised. But never a sign was there of being taught a foreign language.

Within small, back-breaking desks we were seated, and those children who arrived bearing with them the royal banner of Imagination were immediately divested of it. For it was considered unhealthy to possess such a dangerous and wasteful power; a power that has moulded and raised the civilisations of the past; a power that has transmuted the savage known as man into a fairer and cleaner pattern. No, Imagination was poetical, and Poetry was not in the curriculum.

So, within these large rooms, narrow dogmatisms and fragments of learning were forcibly injected into our languid minds; tasteless and brittle stubble garnered from the fields of knowledge and thrown to us by exhausted and nerve-strained teachers, who knew much of little things but little of big things. Teachings regarding deportment, manners, and consideration for others were likewise lacking. For we were the children of parents who were considered the potato peelings, orange skins, shards and general leavings of society. We were not considered truly human, but society had a certain conscience that demanded to be obeyed. Therefore society wasted its money—for waste it certainly was —upon the education of its lower classes. And what a pitiful, unimaginative waste it was. For directly we left school, nearly all was forgotten. And it deserved to be.

There were a few unfortunate children who possessed a personality. This dangerous sign was attacked at once, and strenuous efforts were made to make them as mindless as the rest. All personality was erased and upon the palimpsest were inscribed the standardised views and doctrines of the Educational Board.

For these reasons, though I was unconscious of the reason for my revolt, I hated school. How I hated it! I rarely walked to this dismal place; I was dragged there. And when I sat in my desk, I sat there like a fool. And at playtime I would often stand apart from my playmates brooding like a hurt animal. I never, and now I look upon it with pride, received a prize for regular attendance.

The elastic moods of youth, the quick forgetfulness of sorrow, the spontaneous welcoming of a joyful moment, and the feverish restlessness for a long-awaited event are incidents of the past that one sometimes meditates upon. And my sorrow was the entrance into school; my joyful moment, the release; the long-awaited event, the arrival of a holiday. And though those hours of release brought little of that lyrical quality that should be the heritage of every child, I yet return with some slight regret to that period; for the crystalline quality of mind being lacking, a true understanding of this misery that surrounded me lost much of its poignancy.

I think it is only in adolescence that feelings and thoughts become more intense, more sensitive; afterwards, one becomes used to it all, dulled, fatalistic.

The first few years after my schooling holds for me but little interest. The district in which we lived was much better. But as this is a tale relating to the mind, there is little need to dwell upon these phases.

I entered many trades for but short periods, for I excelled in none, and often committed the fatal mistake of being either too painstaking or dreaming. Only one ideal held me—an ideal possessed and dreamt over ever since childhood: to write a book. I had no other ideal save that one.

Now it was only at the age of eighteen that I really began to think. Previously the days had vanished like a continually moving curtain of mist, teaching me little, and leaving in my mind a debris of uninteresting incident. And even when the faun of adolescence stirred within me and warmed my blood with his passion music, when his melodies ceased, there was little to remember him by. It was only when the thin radiance of thought began to glimmer within mind that I began to realise that I possessed the power to place, in their various apartments, the things and ideas I had previously considered one and indivisible; that I was an individual with power to rebel against accepted concepts and conventions.

How my emotions spluttered and frothed! Ignited by the electrical power of an idea, a new dream, a breath-shaking revelation, I attempted to illuminate and burn with the fire within me those whom I met. But the insulations were faulty; therefore I expressed myself in a series of stammers intermixed with intermittent flashes of brightness. I burned with a destructive fervour. And injustice was frequently the fuel that made me boil over and steam. The spirit of rebellion entered into me and intoxicated me. And with this came the growth of egotism and argumentative, callow cynicism.

But, in my mental birth, I was feebly and primitively equipped, and I had to stumble on alone without the crutches of education to help me onward. Like a would-be knight without armour or steed I endeavoured to journey into the land of thought, bearing only the club of egotism with which to conquer my adversaries. Thus armed, I strode onward, meeting, after a few strides, an Atheist. A middle-aged man dwelling in a stone hut by the wayside. The background being sparse and arid, hill-less and ending in the abyss of utter negation. He was a hermit as primitive and as crude as myself, and he denounced and jeered at the existence of a God, shattering, lustily and lengthily, the beliefs of the Bible on the clumsily built anvil of his convictions. He was a good, simple and sincere man, whose father I believe had been a parson. Conceivably he had reacted against the narrowness of the teachings forced upon him, but that had not made him the less narrow in his reactions.

The society to which this man belonged hated the idea of a God, hated the churches, and hated the priesthood; worshipping instead the teachings of the materialistic-minded scientists. And I believe their characters were just as fanatical and capable of indulging in autos-da-fé and other torments, had they lived in such a period, as the opponents they attacked. For, despite their scientific knowledge, they seemed to be incapable of understanding that it would be as hard to eradicate from these people, who possessed a different consciousness, their knowledge and sense of divine realities as it would be to change the shape of a star. For they squeezed and crushed all knowledge brought to them in the vice of intolerance.

Previously I had believed in God without knowing the existence of other theories. Praying to Him simply and naturally and in perfect faith; not deeming that the interpretations of life were as multitudinous and as various as the leaves on a tree. Not having had any strong religious training, for our parents permitted us to think as we desired, evoking therefore no religious discussion in the home, the theories of my atheistical companion interested me considerably, though at first I was somewhat disturbed, for the bed of my belief was comfortable and warm. But after giving ear to many of his now obviously crude arguments, in which coarse humour was often used as a further nail thrust into the coffin of God, and thinking over much that he said, I accepted his views, not possessing sufficient education or discrimination to reject. From that moment I commenced arguing as vigorously and as absurdly as my newly discovered friend. But, strange to say, blasphemy never became the weapons of my attack.

Now had I become somebody strange and daring. I was an atheist. Not many people I discovered were atheists. I was virile in attack and long words—we favoured long words because they sounded more impressive—floated down like logs of wood from the tongue; also, I was unsparing in the use of my club. All those who disbelieved in me were my enemies, and I attempted to batter in, by sheer strength and weight, their thick, intolerant skulls. Oh what disreputable children we truly were! Seriousness lay upon us like cloaks of lead. If only we had possessed a sense of humour. But that came later.

As yet the mist of philosophy had not enshrouded me. And therefore I did not understand that dogmatism in the realm of thought was absurd. Therefore I stayed with my friend for a considerable time, while he initiated me into ponderous books of popular science, wherein the word *Evolution* was the power that dethroned God. Upon such altars in the temples of evolution these priests of materialism sacrificed all other creeds as fanatically as did the priesthood in the mediaeval ages, not understanding that their worshippers were just as ignorant and just as thoughtless as the worshippers of others in the opposing temples.

Yet I think that they have an important part to play in the journeyings and development of the mental traveller; for they wipe away all the prejudices and superstitions accepted from childhood, without question. From that aspect, my meeting with the atheist was of great value. Though, like others, I rapidly made new prejudices; for character does not alter with the birth of new teachings or theories, and I became a general nuisance to all who opposed me. Laughing to scorn those who rejected my superficial arguments; and being ignored, naturally, by those who understood my youthful state of mind. But those who accepted similar theories treated me seriously. For we considered ourselves intellectually superior to those who grazed upon the plains below.

But after many months I became tired of this stony land, and so I decided to travel still farther. I had been told that beyond the frontier of Atheism stretched a land named Socialism. A wonderful and perfect land; a land of cool and refreshing streams and woodlands that sparkled with the gay music of birds and the light fragrance of a myriad flowers; a land where here perfection radiated from the forms and faces of nobly proportioned men and women; a land of Arcady where all were given equal opportunity to express the highest within them. In short, a fragrant social paradise given to man because of the love that the givers felt in their hearts for all humanity.

So, hopefully, I resumed my pilgrimage. Soon after I came to a long, broad and smooth road of a red colour. Flowers grew by the wayside, which, when I plucked them, I found to be artificial. This astonished me, but I soon forgot as I gazed at the quiet beauty that surrounded me. The sun was just rising, another curious phenomenon; for it never topped the valley towards which I travelled. But it was when turning a corner that the sound of a mighty clamour reached my ears. "This," I exclaimed, "should not be. Alas perhaps a jealous enemy had invaded this land of perfection." So I hurried forward, and the clamour increased, while the clockwork birds that greeted me ceased from singing.

Now ultimately I arrived at the drawbridge of a castle built from scarlet stone. And this castle was besieged by an army who wore uniforms of red, and they made the clamour. From one of them I discovered that those in the castle were of the same blood as those who besieged. But that the besieged had drawn up a certain custom that was not to the liking of those who attacked. Therefore did they battle. These I left, for I did not understand the reason for their quarrel. Thus I travelled farther, and the sounds that rent the air grew more ferocious, but they did not float from those whom I left but from another quarter. And again, when I reached the spot from whence the sound rolled, I found that another battle was in being, and that the cause was of a similar nature to the armies I had just left. Then I joined one of the armies and became a mercenary, for otherwise I could not have travelled onward. For castles lay thickly on the land, and battles occurred daily.

Thus I became an archer, wearing a quiver loaded

with the barbed arrows of argument which I shot forth to all who opposed the particular views I held at that moment.

In this land all the inhabitants were in a continual state of siege, and each castle was surrounded by a red mist. Here I remained for a considerable time, travelling from one castle to another, and endeavouring to discover the reason for the enmity that existed between them all. Many of the soldiers swore that their opponents were dishonest and insincere; others held that certain rites in their churches of Love were blasphemous; others maintained that certain rules laid down by their kings should be obeyed, and others disagreed; and still more believed that their great enemy, The Golden Giant, had paid their opponents to spy upon them. Perhaps these were the reasons why the sun never rose.

It was a realm where Suspicion and Misrule were the true sovereigns, and where the arrows of argument were shot down in a perpetual shower.

Now travelling from castle to castle I eventually came to the borders of this country, beyond which lay the nebulous and dark valleys of Anarchism. And here I discovered the philosophy of the ego-intoxicated Nietzsche and Max Stirner, whose god was the superman of black occultism.

In this night-land the doctrines of self were preached: perfect and undiluted freedom for the individual; an inversion of the true occult ideal, in which man is considered a world, but wherein, before he can attain perfect freedom for soul expression, he must be perfect physically, emotionally and mentally; that is: he must be balanced in every attribute of his being and ever willing to help humanity. The reverse is then the black magician who wars against humanity, but who has also developed power and dark wisdom. Thus we can see that in Anarchism the darker side of liberty for the individual is expressed.

Now the people I met were not at all of a bad nature, and certainly they were much more finely evolved and milder than the Socialist. They were more or less atheistical, and because of that believed that the powers in man were limited. Thus they could only, and did, theorise. The truth was they were more or less philosophers holding almost identical doctrines.

In this realm I threw away my quiver of arrows and exchanged it for the swiftly darting rapier, and I roamed, like the rest, alone. I endeavoured to gather material for an ambitious work entitled: "Egotism: Past, Present and Future." A work that was to be written in three vast volumes to prove conclusively how man had risen through the evolution of Selfishness, and how he would ultimately become a god through a similar development. I did not know at that time that selfishness possesses the seeds of its own destruction, but I mention this literary attempt of mine (which needless to say did not go beyond a few pages of notes) in order to show the mental state and youthfulness of my mind. For even had I had the will to accomplish such a feat, I lacked the knowledge to complete it.

Now the people in this dark land were in a hurry. With the mighty broom of Anarchism we determined to sweep and cleanse the whole world. It was to be a universal spring-cleaning, wherein we were to be the cleaners. In the first place we wanted to destroy all tyrants, or at least put them where they would do the least harm to society. We abolished them by the simple process of passing resolutions for revolutions; unfortunately we did not discriminate between the two words, to us they apparently meant the same. Eagerly we wanted that which would give us comfort and time to think, and we did not realise that other people were satisfied with the existing state of society. Because we were restless we wanted all others to be likewise. And I think that Socialism, Anarchism and all the other destructive forms of belief are the result of a mental adolescence, an adolescence intended for all those who strive to better their own conditions of life. For though we speak of three classes of society, we forget another aspect—that of caste. It is possible, in fact I am certain, that hopelessly mixed in our unripe civilisation, are castes whose worlds of thought are as distinct and as far apart as the stars.

Among these anarchists I awakened my mental youth; a youth anointed with the holy oil of dream; a youth virile and passionate; a youth that shook and whipped the blood into fury at the stupidity and selfishness of class and nation. My mind became like a newly broached casket filled with a strong, burning wine. And thoughts, dreams, visions raced tumultuously within me as a torrent as I became intoxicated through its strength. My soul was as a clenched fist that desired to strike and strike and strike against all the inhumanities that surrounded me.

I was in that Spring that is more passionate, more vital, more than all the other springs through which the soul passes on its pilgrimage. And that was the Spring of ideals; a Spring that is the echo of divine vitality. The crimson banner became my symbol; the symbol of social perfection wherein injustice and inequality and hunger would find no place. And pictures of gracious cities; clean-limbed, regal people; and atmospheres of golden, serene beauty dawned from the ecstasies of my revolutionary moods. The fire of my ideals warmed and comforted me in the midst of a cold and comfortless world. Each ideal was a beacon from which I gathered new fuel and fire to light the hearts and minds of the masses. Being extremely sensitive, I was easily impressed by the sentimental eloquence of every revolutionary orator. And I would boil over in a moment at all the injustices related to me. How indignant I felt. How I would denounce with words of vitriol and hate a party or a politician. Afterwards a sense of humour was born and I became more balanced and finally contemptuous of these people who over-exercised their lungs to an undiscriminating, mindless audience. And also I found that their characters did not possess that golden quality that their theories did. Nevertheless, I plucked from this Spring many beautiful flowers. For beyond all the vagueness and muddle-mindedness of these people stood a good and noble force that would ultimately raise man on to a loftier plane wherein dwelt cleanliness and brightness.

I think society will remain immature as long as man remains immature. For though the tender force of a high dream may stretch down and entwine itself around the heart of man, there are the myriad mirages that distract and bewilder him. And though he may hear a weeping in his heart and an urge to enter into the silence of the Higher Self, he is too weak and too young to translate and understand this divine force that all the prophets and poets of the ages have hearkened to. Instead, often the voice of this dream makes him uneasy, and he plunges still further into things that he can understand. But I believe that dream is the voice of the Higher Self demanding obedience from its human instrument and will not release the heart of man from its tendrils but will compel man to accept, if not by love then by pain, its ideal. And only then will society blossom into maturity.

Therefore, though in those early days I was eager to give to all I met my newly discovered wealth and, further, attempted to force it into the heads of all I met, I soon realised the psychological differences in people and discovered the utter futility of propaganda for those not ready for it. For even if those people followed one's doctrines, the fact that much would not be understood would lead to a state of society more chaotic than harmonious. Likewise, I have been told by my teacher since that it is necessary to let other minds alone, for often their roads of development lie in different directions. The Higher Self knows better than we do what is best for its instrument.

Yet it was through Anarchism that I learnt that each person was a world in which different ways of thinking were as immutable as natural laws. And it was likewise through this conclusion that I left the chaotic and dark valleys of Anarchism and journeyed into the vaster, and in many ways vaguer, realms of Philosophy.

Travelling into the country of the Philosophers, I was compelled to throw away my rapier—of what use the sword of argument to combat a mirage?—and instead, bear a distaff. For here I gathered the uncarded wool of ideas discarded from old and young philosophers who were seated beside their wheels spinning finely spun theories.

What wondrous fabrics were woven! There were

cloths, soft and smooth, spun for patrician, mental bodies; warm and comforting wools for optimistic thinkers; and thin and threadbare materials for the superficial intellectual. And like the others, I sat down and wove for myself a suit. But what queer, assorted cloth came from my loom! What strange tints and threads were blended! It was neither linen nor sackcloth, canvas nor satin. It was a combination of all kinds. And the costume that I wore was a trifle clumsy in the beginning and grotesque to the fashionably clad beholder. But it fitted me well enough to suit my purpose. Though after a while some pieces were taken out and replaced by patches that harmonised more completely to my state of mind.

When I had roamed in the land of Anarchism, I had assumed that beyond its borders lay an unfathomable nothingness, and that my mental evolution had ended, and that the next best thing I could do was to gather as much knowledge as this country possessed. Thus, when I stepped over its borders, laden with the twin beliefs of Atheism and Anarchism, into the land of Philosophy, it was with great doubt and uncertainty, for here all things were of an insubstantial nature. My belief in the greatness of the individual was of little use. "Life," these weavers and spinners said, "may be but an idea spun from intangible substances. The body does not exist, only mind. All is force: matter, time, length, breadth and width are but the boundaries of motion. Man is a mote as unimportant as a speck of dust. Man is a universe and the suns and stars are his dreams." Of what use then were my dogmatisms? For these philosophers proved to me that the very ground upon which I walked was but shaped from mist and quicksand.

Slowly I began to realise how little I really knew.

For far beyond well-trodden pastures of the mild-eyed philosophers, who spent their days unravelling the old patterns of ideas left to them by their dead brothers, re-weaving them into patterns and designs of new theories, lay a vast, shadowy coastline towards which I determined to travel, since these philosophers had melted my materialistic dogmatisms. Now the greater problems of life were set before me. One was the problem of existence. I had believed we were as tapers, moulded by environment, while the wick was kindled by an unconscious, mechanical force, and it burned on until the taper melted and returned to the elements. Life was reasonless, and because of that we were compelled to bring a reason into it; further, suffering was the largesse of life distributed in too generous quantities. "For," we argued, "surely no God would be so cruel as to give pain to His creation?"

I had not yet investigated the phenomena of Spiritualism, nor had I even heard of Theosophy. So the keys to certain problems of existence had not yet been placed in my hands. I saw that Anarchism led to the belief in the power of brute force, physically and mentally. For one can fight for power as brutally on the mental plane as upon the physical. I saw that the use of class war was no true and lasting remedy, for such hate and selfishness would only be productive of still greater disharmony.

Slowly, and ever more deeply, a great mental agony possessed me. An unbearable anguish burned into me. I felt so unutterably weak and futile. Rhetoric and coarse fulmination could not help the miserable beggar, could not dissolve the hate and suspicion each nation hurled at one another. A hate that corroded and blistered the social body and poisoned its blood. The disciples of these reforming creeds were too imperfect themselves. Therefore, though I studied philosophy in order to find an answer that would satisfy me, I did not, and the hungry were still the symbols of the pitiless laws of life. For life itself seemed as a terrible living picture that enrobed the whole earth, whereon forces like giant feet trod and smeared into scarlet splashes all things that breathed.

This state of mind continued for a long time, until one day I met an old Socialist who broached to me the subject of Spiritualism. Though I listened keenly to him, his illogical arguments and illustrations irritated me. I told him plainly that I considered such beliefs absurd, primitive and impossible. I should have known better. Philosophy had proved to me long ago the futility of dogmatism. Nevertheless I attended a séance and was amused and appalled. The picture of apparently sane men and women—especially women—seated earnestly in a darkened room, holding hands and waiting expectantly to hear messages from the spirits of dead friends and relations through the mouths of the mediums, held for me at that time not only a sense of its pathos but also of its humour. It was all very interesting, but these people seemed far too ready to accept as genuine any vague statement that the medium or obsessing entity desired to give. Snatching at each fragment of information as though starving, without question or desire to know whether the food given came from the mind of the medium or truly from a disembodied spirit.

I concluded, from the results of my first visit, that there was too little proof in the study of this subject.

"Still," I thought "it is worthwhile examining the psychological aspect." And it was from that aspect that I attacked these beliefs and strove to find whether there were any scientific justification for this subject. It was while on this quest that I came to the science of hypnotism, and herein I found much more proof about the possible powers of the mind than I had ever yet conceived.

For I never realised what forces lay dormant within the brain until that moment, though later on I was to learn of still greater and more wonderful powers of which certainly the Western students of psychology and hypnotism are ignorant.

A little later on I heard of another theory about life, which was Theosophy. Curiosity led me into a hall where lectures upon such a subject were being delivered; and, while listening to the lecturer, a realisation dawned within me, clarifying all the vague and half-formed intuitions that had glimmered within my mind since childhood. One after another problems began to be solved. The past beliefs of childhood, such as: magic, fairies, religion and God again resumed their sovereignty, though of course the Theosophical terms were different. Thus: fairies were elementals; magic, unknown laws; the Logos, God. But what mattered terms as long as they meant the same? Another reason why I listened so eagerly and accepted much that was said was not because this speaker awakened old and beautiful beliefs but because he was so reasonable, explaining the solution to so many problems. We had lived before, and in our past lives did things that produced reactions in this; hence were all our sufferings not caused by God, but by our own actions. We also had the free-will to do good or evil; those choosing evil learning through suffering to do good, and those doing good learning to become instruments for Divine purposes. And here I will quote a teaching given to me since by my teacher.

The black powers of life are needed, because through opposition man calls out to God for right direction. The seeker is brought into touch with those dark forces in order to give him the power to discriminate between right and wrong action.

Thus, in Theosophy, intelligent, though unfamiliar, reasons were given to explain many things, and in this new world of thought spread before me I determined to banquet. I had a prodigious appetite; nothing was cast away. I digested works in which even Theosophists were not interested. And here and there I found a little titbit that mixed well with the varied and strange foods I discovered. Pamphlets and booklets were my first choice; then came two huge volumes of a work that is treated with a contempt it certainly does not deserve: namely, *The Secret Doctrine* (H. P. Blavatsky)—the most remarkable book, I venture to suggest, of the nineteenth century. But I was compelled to put it aside, as it dealt with subjects much too profound for my understanding; but more elementary works of a kindred nature were read at the rate of about a dozen a week. For I joined the library of the Theosophical Society. The number of books written upon this philosophy are immense. And it was in this library that I had the opportunity of studying the scientific basis for their beliefs; though I know full well that the scientist would not even attempt to study and examine if there is any possible truth in this doctrine. He is much too superior for that. And after all, is not a study of the habits of a beetle of much more importance than an understanding of the spirit of things and of God?

Meanwhile I still attended, in a cursory fashion, the Spiritualist séances and began to get some proofs in a most unpleasant manner. After leaving these circles phenomena would take place when I was alone. I would hear taps and knocks at night, and on one or two occasions I had the unpleasant and uncanny experience of something dragging me out of my body. This gave me unwelcome proof, inconceivable as it may sound to the materialist, that I possessed another form of consciousness within my body; a detachable something that is fully conscious and aware that the body is but a kind of envelope. I can hear the mental specialist and psychologist, who never having had such an experience therefore deny the possibility, murmuring in kind though firm accents that I apparently had some strange form of hallucination—all is a hallucination to the blind and inexperienced and to those who will not see—but nevertheless I maintain that such was an experience that occurred. It was as though something had been unlocked and shown to me, warning me that Spiritualism had its dangers.

Spiritualism, I think, is a land of earnest and unhappy slaves, where many are burdened with strange and miserable creatures, who leer and gibber from the backs of their carriers. Slaves who are weak and half-blind and know not what horrible creatures possess them. It is a land where Curiosity, Grief and Greed are the masters, attracting many voyagers to moor their barques in one of the shadowy havens; a land wherein everything appears distorted; where trees are curiously shaped and unhealthily coloured, their branches grey, writhing and coiling like living things, their foliage thick and glossy with diseased sap; and where even the dark grasses rustle when there is no wind. Here a sombre miasma rises continually from a marshy earth, where the waters of pool and stream are brown and stagnant, save for a radiant brook that flows from a distant mountain range. And this brook is one of those white threads of Truth that run through age to age, through civilisation to civilisation, bringing with it an eternal light, and murmuring an eternal yet ever-changing hymn for those who are willing to see and hear.

Through such a land had I wandered, meeting people who had blindly stumbled through the entangling jungles. For Spiritualism is often a roadless land, wherein to journey is to travel with ears deaf to the wild laughter and howling of unseen hosts; people proud and delighted in being obsessed, being sincere in their beliefs that the spirits possessing their bodies used them for unselfish motives, when quite opposite motives were usually much in evidence. These people desired to be instruments of God, but unfortunately they left the cellar doors of the human house wide open, permitting an invasion of unholy spirits who sometimes reigned supreme. And, though bewilderment and fascination had entranced them, if they had but listened more keenly they would have heard in the distance the frail whisper of the silver stream; and if they had but developed sufficient strength to travel towards it, they would ultimately pass out of the grey and evil mist of this land and enter a country of brighter hues, where the flower-fringed ribbon of light grew broader and flowed into the river that journeyed through the continent named Theosophy.

Incidentally a few remarks from my teacher regarding Spiritualism may be of interest:

The child must take its first steps in the attainment towards the realisation of Truth; and in its stumbling often wanders into the mazes underlying Spiritualism as it is understood. But a pure mind and heart will lead him through this land of mist and bewilderment into the world of the soul's awakening. Therefore he should not be condemned if he is sincere, for there are many paths to God.

So these experiences prepared me to accept much that the Theosophists claimed, and I learned that in seeking and discovering there is no end. The mental vistas broaden daily; wider and wider grow the fields of knowledge, for every inch of space and air teems with invisible intelligences of a most wonderful and varied nature, titanic as well as minute.

DIVINE ECHOES

The past is a dark power that would entwine its coloured strands around the impatient feet of the traveller. It is a divine ghost that should sleep unstirred by those who would know God in a new guise. Do not listen to the sad echoes of its ancient grandeur or bereave its loss. The arcadian beauty of Greece has been woven into your blood; the massive dusk of Egypt and her profound gods are part of your strength; the indomitable force called Rome still moves you onward. The dumb and sand-lapped cities—those labours of colossal thought —will again be rebuilt upon a yet vaster scale. Do not mourn the old. If those monumental works have been sacrificed to the hours, it is because the great Architect has new moulds to shape. If the brazen cymbals that once invoked the gods clang no more, it is because a mightier and more majestic music is to be born in the new period when the gods will again awaken, bringing still greater gifts and wonders for man. Remember that within you dwell the blended echoes of the centuries.

CHAPTER TWO

THEOSOPHY

There is a belief among certain people that Theosophy is a nonsensical and primitive conception of the universe, invented by a clever charlatan named Madame Blavatsky. This is utterly untrue. Theosophy is as old as the universe, for it deals with the spiritual aspect of Nature—the causes of phenomena instead of merely the effects—and explains to us the spiritual meaning of life, the reasons for our sufferings and the cure. Theosophy possesses a great ethical force and is clear-cut and as scientific from its own standpoint as any branch of modern science, except that it deals with the interior world of the soul as well as the outer. It does not deny the necessity of material things but helps us to master them. It is like the mouth of a great golden river with innumerable streams whose names are: Spiritualism, Magic, Astrology, Psychology, Folklore, and a host of beliefs accepted by the majority of the Eastern nations; and among them the law of Reincarnation is one of the chief bases for all the other aspects.

Such was the world of thought into which I willingly and gladly entered. Besides a clear explanation of the causes of much of our suffering, it restored many of the romantic ideas my imagination had played with since I was a child. The realisation that Justice was not merely a man-made conception but a natural law gave me a great mental relief. The evil we send out returned to us as inexorably as the good. Emotional, mental and physical forces all had their reactions. In the knowledge gained later, I actually found this to be demonstrable. Even Science admits the truth of telepathy, a mental force that can annihilate space like wireless, and which if carefully investigated, could act similarly with time. Man, I think, possesses an unlimited consciousness, but he himself has limited himself and lives now in an extremely narrow range of consciousness. However, he is today using his mind to a greater extent than in the past few centuries, hence the reactions which we call nervous diseases. For man has not yet realised that he can receive blows mentally and emotionally, as well as physically. This is an experience I have often had in the last few years, as my occult training has made me more and more sensitive; and I think it is quite possible that as mankind generally grows more sensitive he will begin to realise how one can be attacked on the subtler realm of mind by mental criminals; so that a new method will be discovered of punishing these mental criminals, as those are punished who perpetrate physical crimes.

In Theosophy I found I could place in various apartments many of the problems that had puzzled me when I had travelled through the realms of my mental adolescence, for the solutions offered by Atheists, Socialists and Anarchists were only moral medicines administered to the physical body by doctors who were two-thirds blind. Though I had discarded their suggestions for the cure of crippled man, I could still sympathise with them, for I realised that from their outlook they were perfectly sincere; but their mental sight being somewhat blurred, they saw much more vaguely than many of their patients and, therefore, were liable to inflict upon their unwilling victims more sufferings than cures. Yet it is not the Socialist who is to be blamed for his materialistic outlook but the sceptical scientist who has denied too readily much that other people have discovered, including even the experiences of a few scientists in certain investigations of psychical phenomena.

Equally blameworthy are the societies who have published cheap works in vast numbers, written by these sceptics, and placed them in the hands of semi-illiterates, who have never had the opportunity to investigate for themselves the apparent truths laid down by these sceptics. And I had been in a similar position, for I had to accept blindly, until I rebelled, all that these cheap and often badly written works had affirmed. Hence I cannot blame the Socialist for his pessimistic outlook but rather his masters, the sceptical scientists. I think the elementary schools should teach, as the most important foundation for mind-training, a simple form of philosophy, showing in the first place the insubstantiality of things; how even the scientist only deals with the effects and not the causes, proving that all is uncertain and that our senses are very imperfect instruments. The result would be that for many years the mind would not indulge in dogmatisms but would listen to all things and weigh them carefully. Nowadays, such a training can only be had in universities, when all schools should possess it.

In the Theosophical Society I met a number of people with whom I quickly became friendly. Interesting people, some who had had certain psychical experiences and some who hoped to have them, among whom of course was myself. Question upon question poured from me, and the more I studied the numerous works in the library the more I realised how little mankind generally knew of the anatomy of the soul. I studied strange books of philosophy that melted any dogmatic assertion I cared to make and books upon hypnotism that proved to me the terrible and hidden powers locked up in the mind of man; they showed me the dangers that surrounded humanity and the true remedies; and, finally, the manner whereby man could become godlike and filled with wonderful knowledge. Yet what they revealed above all were the difficulties that man must face if he would transmute his weakness into strength; into sacrifice, selflessness, renunciation of all that is evil; and into sincere desire to be an instrument working in harmony for the good of all.

But reading alone was certainly not sufficient. "Live the philosophy," repeated itself continually in my mind. "And avoid too many intellectual arguments. Criticism destroys more than it constructs." For at this period, despite my adoption of a lofty belief, the delight of overcoming a mental opponent in an intellectual battle brought me into considerable disrepute among those who were more mystically inclined. Friends who moved in the serene air of unthinking faith disliked me. I disturbed their habitual calm. But they also irritated me, for they accepted far too much without thinking, and I still believe they were much too sentimental and fatalistic. The fact that Truth gleamed from a mountain peak, and that we saw this gleam, should have made us more eager to scale the heights, instead of accepting the fact in a negative spirit, which I am afraid many did. But I was restless; my mental feet had carried me to the coastline of Philosophy, and now it remained for me to voyage onward. Therefore, I could not tolerate the mental weariness of my friends.

Realisations were necessary if my studies were to be of any use. So I immediately became a vegetarian—not very difficult for me, for I had never been overfond of meat—though how far it gave me spiritual realisations I have never discovered. I have met many vegetarians, but rarely do they seem to have experienced anything of a supernormal nature. At odd moments I also tried to concentrate and meditate, but the results were not at all impressive. I received no startling visions, nor did I have the experiences gained in the strange atmosphere of Spiritualism.

Yet I journeyed on, studying now and then the huge volumes of *The Secret Doctrine*, understanding but little of it, though drinking all in, puzzled, enthusiastic. I found I could not gain much, though I believe I was as sincere as any member. It was not due to lack of effort; but I felt as though a great wall stood between me and the wonderful phenomena, written about in the numerous books, which I was not big enough to climb. For though I knew there were certain methods of gaining first-hand knowledge, I did not desire to awaken any force I would not be able to control. Nor did I care at that time for the teachings of other occult schools which lacked the aspects I desired. Meanwhile I stayed within the Society, steeping myself in the teachings and endeavouring spasmodically to understand. Nevertheless, all the time I was shaping for myself a clearer and finer philosophy of life, gathering a thread here and there and weaving it into an ideal pattern, which I hoped would be of use in the future years of existence.

Here my chief friends were likewise sincere students. Some who practiced and had achieved results of a temporary nature, many of their experiences being similar to my own in Spiritualism, for being sensitive they could very quickly get unpleasant proofs of the darker side of phenomena. We gathered often in a small dark room over an antique shop in Soho to exchange ideas, to meditate, to grumble at the uselessness of life and to hope for the best. Here I met David, who was to become my partner and companion in many spiritual and material ventures, and a fellow-pilgrim in the quest of realisation. He introduced me to a group of other students; and, as some have been my companions ever since and have attempted the same spiritual pilgrimage as myself, I shall endeavour to describe them.

David was of short and somewhat slight stature; pale and intensely sensitive (he originally disliked me because I was too crude and argued with him); serious; and, I used to think, much too casual about the incidents of this world, and much too deeply engrossed in the world within. He always appeared to move in a perpetual haze. He had had some most interesting experiences of an occult nature when young, which helped me to prove the existence of unknown states of consciousness, and when I first met him his air of other-worldliness puzzled me greatly. I remember particularly one day, when I was waiting for him in the shadow of a staircase, he touched me to see if I was real or a ghost. Life to him was then very insubstantial, although since that period he has had experiences which have taught him the wisdom of planting his feet firmly on earth. He strove to live the mystical life and gave to every beggar he met his last few pence. Unfortunately, the people to whom he gave were sometimes the least deserving. In fact, his mystical life did not develop the power of discrimination; a characteristic I have noticed among many who live in too mystical an atmosphere. The occultist with true understanding does not give his love to all, for there are some whom, if given love, would return it with hate; but the reason for this I will mention in a further chapter.

The mystic generally overflows with a sentimentality of a most unbalanced form, and it is fortunate for him he is not wealthy, for any rogue could very quickly drain him dry. He is the mystical fool of God who has to learn Balance, Discrimination and Understanding. Since that time we have learned by painful experience the necessity for these qualities. With the exception of one or two practically all our small group were unbalanced in one way or another. Although the majority of mankind are similarly afflicted, this group had developed a certain form of neuroticism that we labelled unconventionality and bohemianism. We prided ourselves on the fact that we were not as other mortals, and I am certain that other mortals, seeing our group walking and hearing them talking, would feel pleased to believe they were not as ourselves. Still, I think bohemianism appeals secretly to all.

Another friend was an Irishman; dark, of medium height and well-built; quick-tempered, argumentative, and somewhat of an orator, a gift he had used many times during a life spent in world wandering. He was the oldest member of the group and generally looked upon as the leader. Very intolerant of the small conventions and quite brusque in conversation, despising fools, he associated with us because he knew we were sincere students, even if we were unpractical. Though he possessed many fine qualities, I still think he placed the habit of independence upon too high a pedestal. I have mentioned this because I noticed that, among other characteristics, independence (which too often means a swollen egotism) was very much in evidence in our small company. This Irishman had travelled in many countries and is still doing so, yet he keeps in touch with us. For though we may often part, yet being illumined by the same passion and desire of transmuting and purifying the common clay into a finer habitation for the spirit, we never forget one another. He was much older than we were, and had had many interesting adventures and psychical experiences which he would often relate to us. He had been an editor and a lecturer, an engineer and an author; and knew something of many other professions.

The next member of the group was a young Frenchman named Paul; a slim and curly haired youth, artistic and impulsive, who collected odd characters as a hobby. The plain and common-sense person never appealed to him. They had to be erratic and eccentric and, above all, poor. Suffering generally from a form of neurosis, they came, afflicted us for a short time, borrowing all that we could possibly give and vanishing like bad dreams. Personally, I gave little to these persons and thought them unhinged and very unhealthy; since then I have found no reason to change my mind, for they are people whose irresponsibilities have caused more anger in a week than a normal person causes in a year. They are as unreliable as the wind, and had we had them for too long a time among us we ourselves would have become as neurotic and impossible as they. It was noticeable that after a short time the air of the places they visited became charged with a subtle force that was exceedingly unpleasant. One's nerves became strained and one's imagination heightened. But, unfortunately, Paul delighted to bring them along, exaggerating their charms and genius and truly believing that because they were different, they were therefore better. Paul, like the rest of us, was also very sensitive and would argue with the others, who studied Buddhism, about the illusions of existence. He continually chanted the well-known Indian dirge, "All is Illusion; all is illusion; all is illusion." And here I think dwelt the explanation of our lassitude: for Life did not matter, money did not matter, marriage did not matter, the whole objective universe did not matter; all being illusion. God gave us eyes to blindfold and ears for deafness. In short, complicated and wonderful attributes of being were ours merely to be shattered and obliterated, which I think is not the true doctrine of any great religion.

To obey these negative beliefs may have been excellent in India, where the inhabitants voluntarily fed the priests; to obey them in the Western countries would result in our being arrested as beggars. I think each country has the religion best fitted for it; and if we incarnated in the West, it was in order to give the personality a new experience. For though we were Europeans we all strongly believed in rebirth. The greatest desire of the group, with the exception of myself, was to visit India and Tibet, dwell in the jungle, and by meditation ultimately attain Nirvana; a state of spiritual consciousness that was, I believe, little understood. I have heard many Theosophists, argue about it, for to some it apparently meant the total annihilation of every sense and form of consciousness, and I imagined that the Atheist had, from that aspect, as good a conception as any unphilosophic Buddhist student. I thought that this obliteration-of-being an ideal (to which we were to sacrifice all things) of much less worth than the desire of the sincere Christian who wished to become an instrument of God. And at that time I really could not understand that aspect of life, although I now see it was my misunderstanding of Buddhist doctrine. Hence I could not understand such a passion for India. I was much more attracted to the romance of these beliefs, and also I considered that our sincere motives were surely sufficient, if, of course, we lived accordingly to our highest aspirations. But I was treated as a Philistine, a clumsy creature who did not possess the Oriental subtlety of mind or sufficient sentiment of heart; that I had somehow stumbled into a world much too rare and ethereal for one of my order. Furthermore, I was much too interested in literature to be spiritual. I was too incoherent in my questions, and I wanted proof. I wanted occult demonstrations which I never received. And, finally, I delighted in hair-splitting arguments. My mind had eaten so much that it was difficult to digest all the mental food, neither could I systematise all the philosophical facts and theories. But I remained with this group because I had never met so many strange people before, and they fascinated me. It should be remembered that I had arrived from the stony land of Atheism and the red realms of Socialism, where the people were more or less of a commonplace type; while here I found friends of a new mental species altogether.

I have only mentioned three of my friends, for we have all travelled more or less together upon similar roads. The rest were as so many passing shadows, leaving little to be remembered after they disappeared.

My progress in the Theosophical Society continued, and, having imbibed many of the conceptions, I began to attend a local lodge; listening to the lectures and arguing about my beliefs with my old Socialist friends, who now thought me slightly insane for ceasing to sing the well-known and somewhat frayed ditties of Socialism, and replacing them with the wild and weird strains of Spiritualism and Theosophy, which were not at all acceptable to their "rational" point of view. The idea of a new form of consciousness-after-death was greeted with laughter and jeers. They had used their minds to think in only one way and they could not, or would not, trouble to look upon life from an entirely different aspect. They imagined because these theories were so old they were therefore untrue; yet many things we dismissed with a sneer years ago are being accepted today. "Let us," the Socialists would say to me, "first alter the structure of society by erecting the ideal state of Socialism. Food is of more importance than faith; look how mankind suffers. Man is moulded by his environment, and only a change of society can alter his character." This I thought only partly true, as the pressure of environment is weaker or stronger according to the type of individual. The mentally strong man can rise above his conditions as easily as the purely physical type succumbs—the strong soul treating its environment as wax upon which it impresses its personality. So, often if a man lives in bad surroundings, it is because he has little aspiration to travel higher; also from the aspect of reincarnation we make our environment for the future in accordance with the actions of our past lives. It is also probable that the spirit within us forces us into bad surroundings in order to develop our strength, and who knows but that the soul in a previous incarnation came from a lower sphere, where conditions existed far worse than those of this planet. I have been told by my teacher that there are spheres below this Earth wherein the atmosphere is always twilight, and the faces of these souls are of a leaden hue. How many people inhabiting the slums have a desire to make their homes cleaner and brighter? Therefore, one may give quite a number of reasons to prove that man is not such a slave as the sentimentalists and Socialists would have us believe, though it is obvious that none welcomes pain and misery; and, wherever possible, we should try to help humanity. In a later chapter I will mention how the occultist interprets the need of serving mankind.

As I plunged more deeply into the woods, meadows, and sometimes jungles of Theosophy, I lost touch with my old acquaintances of the immature mental journeyings. For I desired to go further with my search, while they were satisfied that truth had already been found and that little could be discovered in what they considered "going back to old superstitions and religions"; in fact, they thought this to be a form of mental degeneracy.

One thing that amazed me was the number of small societies teaching occultism and mysticism, most of them being offshoots of Theosophy. Modern Rosicrucianism, Buddhism and Gnosticism, Christian Mysticism and Indian Yoga all found plenty of exponents. With regard to Yoga, I would utter a warning to those who, misunderstanding its true teachings, try to practice the occult science of Breath, either for self and gain or without proper supervision; for they may sometimes awaken powers beyond their control and that would do much more harm than good. Fortunately, most people did not have sufficient perseverance to continue these practices; also many wanted to develop powers merely to boast how different they were from others. Here I have noticed how quickly and eagerly the most materialistic person will listen to somebody who states that he can tell the future or read hands. Immediately they meet such a person out shoots the palm, and answers are eagerly awaited. Servant girls are not the only superstitious species, for there appears to dwell in the heart of everybody a desire to know the future and a secret belief or hope that such futures can be foretold. From practical experience I have found that this is really possible, but not by visiting a charlatan who merely states what the client wishes. For, as my teacher has instructed me, things of a spiritual nature must not be used for personal gain. Otherwise, a time will come when the clairvoyant will be illusioned by his own Higher Self, bringing him probable disgrace, for the soul will not prostitute its wares in the marketplace. That is a law for all the disciples on the Path and for those who are not, for wherever readings of the future are to be bought for money, the person "seeing" will not be able to speak from the highest source. Still, I believe there are methods of divination, such as astrology and palmistry, which are permissible. Nevertheless, the susceptible should be careful about wishing to know the future, as it can sometimes lead to a very unhealthy state of mind. For thought has the power to shape our actions, and the fortune-teller can sometimes hypnotise us into bringing about the events he has foretold. That is one of the reasons why the genuine clairvoyant says very little and hides the gift, if possible, unless he is told to help somebody. Then he gives freely and without thought of money or return.

I have visited many of the smaller mystical societies, and though I found them interesting, I never desired to join them. I always felt that these organisations did not possess the *realisations* of the truths about which I had read so much. I accepted the fact that they all possessed some form of truth but questioned whether they had reached the highest, which alone I sought. Not that I had had any experiences of a spiritual nature, for many years were to pass before I received demonstrable teachings.

So I waited and studied continually the philosophies of the various schools, feeling that if I lived according to the highest within me I would ultimately find that for which I had sought so long and often despairingly.

Here my friends also remained; David sometimes studying astrology, generally wandering about as though caught in the misty maze of a dream; Paul returning from his voyages of discovery in the strange underworld of Bohemia with an important capture, usually a weird and vague artist, male or female, impressing us with the genius of the said being, whom we worshipped for at least a week. Then, getting weary, we would dismiss the fading star for another unrecognised luminary of the heavens, who accepted our homage with a matter-of-fact air. While all the time the Irishman grumbled at life, and we with him.

THE CHIMERA OF CLAY

The false lustre of Earthly existence entices the senses of the discarnate spirit to wrap its subtle body in the folds of temporary clay that at first is fragile and faintly perfumed with echoes of scent blown from the sweet flowers of the heavenly meadows. But, slowly, the rare atmosphere that enveloped the young fades away, as the unseen waves of the world dash against the body and mould and beat into the trembling flesh the vices, the habits, the moods of life, until the delicate petals droop and are twisted into a distorted blossom. The apparent rich beauty and brook-ensilvered lawns that allured the simple spirit to this realm dissolve into a jungle, teeming with lustful beasts; and, amid this pandemonium, the soul, becoming intoxicated by the Lethean wine of living, loses remembrance of its holy state.

CHAPTER THREE

THE JUNGLES OF MAYA

Most evenings of the week being free; we visited the cafés of Soho, where Queen Bohemia in her motley holds court, her music being the overture to the drama entitled: "Drink, Drugs and Delirium." With painted face and bedraggled peacock's tail, she struts through all the scenes, singing from a leering mouth in a harsh, cracked voice feebly written hymns to Bacchus and Venus. In recalling to mind these places, the impressions awakened are of atmospheres close and heavy; glaring inharmonious colours; faces pale, bloodless and painted, the imprints and marks of dishevelled souls; forms flaccid and drooping (such being a sign that one was artistic); mild and stolid faces of suburban adventurers; artistic faces, artless faces and artful faces, or, as a friend once said, places where the artless fed the artful. They were like mental jungles where the mental ape, the lion, the fawn, the elephant, the tiger, wolf and screeching parakeet mingled promiscuously and quarrelsomely. An atmosphere that insidiously perverted the visitors if they were weak or stayed too long, for when I recollect the many people who had made such spots their homes and had failed in their ambitions, I am appalled. To be a visitor once or twice is an interesting experience; to visit them more often would be disastrous.

Here the artistic lion would hold his salon: someone generally more notorious than artistic, seated in state, with his mental mane smoothed and combed by his admirers, holding the sceptre of egotism which he would hurl at those who had the audacity to question his high degree. For in these places egotisms grew as rapidly as toadstools, and the flames of jealousy were often kindled in the hearts of those who desired to be seated in the throne of the local lion.

The subjects of these little kingdoms had accomplished many things, but unfortunately one could not see their works of art. For they had been hung in the great halls, palaces, academies and exhibitions of the vast realm of "Tomorrow," a country cloyed with the most superb of masterpieces and where every artist was a lion whose mane was greater than all others; a land where each possessed a harem of gentle and humble lionesses who obeyed the faintest roar of their lord swiftly and without question; where statues were erected that excelled in height the mountains; and where the birds, the winds, the rivers sing and murmured the praises of the kingly inhabitants.

We visited these places for a number of reasons. Paul because he desired to meet strange people; David because he hoped to become acquainted with those who had mystical beliefs; the Irishman for amusement; and myself to meet literary people, and finally as a change from our own commonplace homes. Paul very rapidly found those he was seeking. David met a few dreamers. The Irishman got all the amusement he could wish for. But, alas, I found little. Literature did not dwell here, though there were many modern versifiers whose scorn for Shakespeare only excelled my scorn for their verse: lines generally lacking in music, colour, imagination, technique and thought; lacking, too, in inspiration, though that nowadays does not matter. For much so-called inspiration comes from unrestrained emotion I was told, although it was true that inspired poetry was picturesque and in many childlike ways delightful, only much, much too religious. Such were the ideas often expressed to me by a varsity man, one Lancelot Hoity Highface, an editor, I understood, of a modern publication entitled *The Ice Box*, a biennial for the moderns.

He was a tall, slender man; languid, somewhat pale and handsome in a classic and cold way; and his words were high-pitched, slow and perfectly enunciated. Many of the poems I saw in his publication reminded me of wingless, defeathered sparrows with broken or crippled legs, causing them to hop in a curious and clumsy fashion. As for the articles, they gave me the impression of a waterless journey across a vast and arid desert.

I also met many journalists, but I found them to be singularly uninterested in literature, though of course I may be mistaken; probably they did not desire to speak about such things, being surrounded by print all day. So I must confess that I received little intellectual food, though I could have suffered with a surfeit of the emotional diet offered.

To attempt to describe the interiors of these cafés would be to describe the materialised dream of a diseased mind. Here the psychoanalyst could have found more material in one small room than in any large district, for many of the walls were stained with pictures imaging vague and chaotic states of thought. There lay an indescribable ugliness, the result of much disgusting talk and tales, that gave the air a certain heaviness; certainly not alleviated by the profuse smoke and the smell of stale beer.

Here our little group would sit and watch the fantastic pageant, drinking from thick glass-tumblers weak and highly priced Russian tea; and listening to the loud, shaggy voices of women and low-pitched, giggling, sexual laughter of young students and frowsily clad men. Sometimes the rooms were painted throughout in black—black tables, black ceilings, black walls and black doors; painted, I understand, to still the troubled moods of the artistic souls. Sometimes the rooms were coloured in pink, green, yellow, red and every possible tint in the form of lozenges, pyramids, diamonds, spirals, circles, squares—all shapes that the mind could imagine. Sometimes they were perfectly bare. Others were enriched with futuristic pictures of an incomprehensible nature, the two-dimensional incarnation of an innate and shadowy thought. Or possibly one could describe them as hysterics objectified into paint, hurriedly wrenched from the abyss of chaos and hurled violently and savagely upon the walls. These pictures would be proudly shown to us, and the names of the Painters would be whispered with bated and awestruck tones (generally a person who was a drunkard or drug-taker). We, not being artists, listened and had to accept as fact that these works were wonderful, for we were afraid to criticise. After all, we were but philistines. And now I think nearly all the people in these cafés were philistines but were afraid to confess the truth that the work was detestably bad and of a most unhealthy nature. I think we made a virtue of astigmatism, and anyone suffering from this disease, and striving to paint or write, was hailed as a coming genius, simply because he produced something crooked instead of straight, imagining a crooked line was better than a curve. Because such a thing had not been done by the truly great artists, their originality gave them admission into the Pantheon of art. The truth of the matter was that their astigmatic souls but increased their egotism.

We noticed that few of the women were artists, and I think many were there in order to inspire some of these disciples of art. What these women did for a living was a mystery. Some I understood were models; others actresses and dancers; and many lived with artists and suffered for it. Sometimes a genuine artist would enter, but not be such a spendthrift of hours as the pseudo-artists. Such a man would be too busy working to spend too long a time in these places. There seems to be a legend that if a person is an artist he must therefore be a degenerate, make a thorough beast of himself, seduce every woman he meets, and end his life by drinking himself to death. It is true that an artist is obviously more emotional and sensitive than the normal person, and he swiftly reacts to his environment; but to become an artist he must surely develop strength of character in order to study and complete his works, and that in itself should and does give him the necessary control and training to withstand the degenerating influences that surround him. It is significant that when he does work he often tries to dwell in the country or on the Continent where he can have peace for his task; while the artists met in these cafés were often weak and inefficient and generally worked not because they were inspired or in love with their art, but in order to earn more money for drink or drugs.

Many visitors came because they were curious and desired to know how the artist lived, returning home with a totally wrong conception; others came because they imagined it to be daring and unconventional, generally mentioning in later years that they were once bohemians and had been personally acquainted with some celebrities (whom they had probably seen sitting at the opposite end of the room and with whom they did not dare converse). Many came because they were utterly weary of the standardised city in which they dwelt. For the heart and mind hungers for a change, wherein colour, romance and gallantry, love and passion all play their parts. To the occult and mystical student, adventure and romance teems in every street and house, but the majority of mankind will not or cannot see below the apparent commonplaces the noble and evil forces that play upon the most insignificant of men. Hence, seeing little of interest and unable to bring beauty into their own environment, they visit these cafés or night-clubs to find that colour which their own world lacks; where one can doff the straight-jacket of convention and don the costume of clown and columbine.

Nowadays, we move in the rigid and unswerving route of habit, reigned over by their majesties King Monkey and Queen Parrot, who sit stiffly upon the hard throne of convention. So that we fear to step from our accustomed places in case the watchful eyes of their Majesties discover our actions and their raucous voices scream out to all their loyal subjects to rend us if we do; and if we are too strong, to boycott us. So men, fearing convention, fearing to do those things that their hearts tell them should be done, visit these cafés to express the hampered desires repressed in the atmosphere of their homes. For nobody is more merciless than the inquisitors of gossip, whose drab world of mediocrity surrounds us: it is a subtle form of hell wherein those who have offended are continually scorched until the heat parches the victim's soul and renders it bloodless, an emaciated pariah that walks tortured by those who never had the courage to express their own convictions.

Our lives are too well ordered. In the morning we digest without thought the petty and hastily written news items; we enter the standardised train or bus and travel the similarly uninteresting and inartistic roads;

we tread the same regularly shaped pavement stones, standardised and square; pass the monotonous row of street lamps, grey, standardised and glaring, the flashy hoardings, and the horrible lines of iron railings that stand so erect like prim and narrow hypocrites. As Samuel Butler wrote in his book *Erewhon*, the result of too much machinery is to become enslaved to machines, and this I believe has occurred. We have become mastered by the machine; our handicrafts, those arts that once brought a healthy pleasure to the beauty-loving eye, have been almost destroyed and The Machine is now enthroned. Only by revolt against its production of non-essential things can mankind be released from its powers.

So in Bohemia we met all those souls that were weary of their standardised world. Only later did we realise the sham that lay beneath this way of escape, though this game of pretence did us little harm, for we perceived the dangers of permitting our weakness to grow and ultimately overwhelm us. It was quite clear to us, from the little we knew of occultism, that many of these artists were obsessed, that they saw clairvoyantly what the drunkard sees in delirium tremens: picturesque, colourful yet nauseating things; and that they had lost their wills and were but open doors to the astral—victims of the unseen and unhealthy forces of evil. But though we knew and understood the spirit of these places, yet we persisted in visiting them until the time came when we lived in our own rooms in Bloomsbury and attempted to carry out our own conceptions of unconventionality and freedom.

THE TORCHBEARERS

In these immortal woods the stately dwellers, who are so youthful, are as eternal fountains of tenderness; and their childlike and meditative faces are troubled by the faint yet passionate echoes of the weeping Earth. And as they tread as gently as the fearless deer that move and browse by their side, they question and pray to the beautiful gods, whose homes are in the mountains, for understanding and power to intercede and destroy the parasitic plants of evil that outstretch their thick, grey tendrils round the souls of our world. And the deep-eyed gods murmur from their azure-bounded pantheons: "If you would lose the light of these quiet havens and become blind to our presences, see no more the dwellers of the perfect stars and become deaf to the melody of their royal voices; if you would deaden your senses and hide the holy fire of your being in red fibres of living clay and be whirled like helpless leaves in the swift, angry breath of that globe—you may salve its mourners."

And these pure ones forsake the brook-lit, velvet glens; the restful music of the trees; the dove-haunted, archaic Temples, wherein are wafted the elusive odour of shy flowers. Leaving the wondering fairy folk and the large-eyed deer, they flow down the viewless heavy currents into the marshes and mazes of a living death.

CHAPTER FOUR

THE MEETING

The period during which we visited the cafés was
also marked by our great devotion to Theosophy. Yet,
though mentally satiated, we had not received any realisations regarding the occult powers of the soul; we
believed strongly in the existence of the inner world
and listened keenly to lecturers who claimed hidden
knowledge, though I admit they rarely spoke about the
possession of supernormal faculties, for generally their
knowledge was based upon certain principles laid down
in *The Secret Doctrine*, and books written by the leaders
of the Society. We met only one man who spoke to us
upon certain powers that he possessed, and he was not
a lecturer or well-known, but he gave some demonstrations proving to us that there were things that could
not be easily explained away by science.

Otherwise, all was talk, beautiful, sentimental and
idealistic talk; conversation upon love, beauty and mysticism, devotional and emotional. We fed our souls with
spoonfuls of mist. One heard in the Society whispers of
initiations, adepts, masters, prophecies of the coming
of a world-teacher, and also small scandals and gossip.
Some members claimed a superiority over others, by the
fact that their incarnations of a hundred thousand years
ago were published in the Society's journal; though why
these supposed lives should have been published I have
never understood. Probably I was jealous because our
little group were little-known; though we were treated
kindly but aloofly, no leader of the Society troubled to
find out what we were doing a million years ago, and
I have always felt somewhat aggrieved regarding that

important matter. In short, the members of the Society were as human as the members of any other society, and in looking back I now realise that spiritual truths and realisations can be found in any quarter of the globe; and the saying, "When the pupil is ready, the Master appears," is perfectly true. I also know that a genuine initiate would never claim superiority over the humblest person, although certain members of this Society did, for the true initiate knows that the humblest seeker may possess some knowledge of which he is ignorant. Also, I think we discussed things too much and eventually lost ourselves in a wood of words; our wanderings led us away from the source of things into the swirling vapours of bewilderment. We studied much that did not really matter, until all was like a perfumed wind and delightful haze; meanings were twisted, spattered and squeezed until they became unrecognisable. Yet we stayed on in the Society because we were enchanted by the shadows and emotional fountains that played upon our senses, becoming more and more somnolent; and it was a long time after that we were forced to admit that all we could learn was of an intellectual nature, which could only lead us into a perpetual mirage. For, above all, what we really desired were realisations that would enable us to comprehend the meanings of life, to understand why humanity suffered; and the cure. For we no longer believed that life woke from the unconscious passions of the elements to snarl and tear its way up a staircase built from the bones of lesser lives.

Only youth, not troubling to dive deeply into the tarns of thought, and the light laughter of pygmy minds who accept and live upon the theories of past great men, will deny an inner meaning to the pains of mankind. And it was for that reason that we left the rocky coast of appearance and sailed, driven by the winds of aspiration, uneasily into the nebulous and fantastic seas of religion, hoping to discover the immortal Hesperides. As I have previously mentioned, we had landed upon the weird shores of Spiritualism and travelled into the kingdom of Theosophy; and though we imagined that here we had found all we wanted, later on even this world of Theosophy that was so tremendous and dealt with so many aspects of life became but a minute fragment of a still vaster continent. And who knows but even this farther land, into which my teacher has led me, is again but a small kingdom leading to regions where even the angels of stars feel as faltering children stumbling to yet mightier continents of knowledge.

And so again we became dissatisfied. We had discovered a number of new conceptions, and now it remained for us to realise those teachings which we had studied so eagerly. For, after all, only when the soul can demonstrate certain truths to its own satisfaction can it really accept those truths; otherwise it must continually hunger until it becomes parched and hopeless. Then in its agony it cries out to God; and probably this may explain why we come to this planet as to a school, where the children feast their eyes and minds upon a myriad dissolving pictures and glamours that pat and fill the camera of the brain with a debris of half-erased recollection. The soul is then forced through thirst and starvation to call out to its body that it also must be fed, until the body is compelled to hearken to its clamour and the mind is withdrawn from the magnetism of the outer visions to listen to the voice of the soul that has cried out for a realisation of God, Truth and Freedom.

For those reasons we began to feel restless and visited other schools of mysticism and occultism that were small but numerous in their diversity of teachings. Like so many hucksters in the marketplace they shouted out the beauty of their spiritual wares; some were costly and some were cheap, some were highly and garishly decorated, and some were primitive and simple. There were mental contortionists and conjurers who juggled and used all possible arts in order to gain money. Yet some were quite honest and certainly had a few truths to give; but the majority bartered. We could learn all about the divine mysteries for so many pounds or dollars; if we increased our payments we could become initiates, whilst he who had the largest pocket became a master, though I expect only a millionaire could become a logos.

Some were small peddlers with peculiar and sometimes unhealthy knick-knacks upon their boards, who furtively whispered the excellence of their wares. Some shouted that they had seen God, but their vices contradicted that possibility—their God may have been a satyr or some perverting elemental. Some spoke about love, but the form of love we suspected they possessed was a love for money. Others told us to leave all the other dealers, for they alone possessed the truth. Still others swore that their competitors were black magicians. Here and there one said that he did not ask for money as he lived upon faith; generally he was the best clad and stoutest of all these dealers. And some plainly threatened us, vowing that if we did not buy from them we would be burnt in an eternal hell after God had destroyed the wicked, among whom of course would be ourselves: a form of blackmail that civilisation has ignored.

There were dealers greasy with self-satisfaction; dealers who puffed ambition; dealers who smirked; and dealers who leered, grotesque in their remedies.

There were some unbalanced, and others balanced with a coldness so scientific that we were repelled by the lack of feeling. Though our logical minds required reason and science yet we desired with them a sense of compassion; on the other hand, the extreme teachings relying upon feeling alone lacked the intellectual power which should expound what was being taught. Yet despite all these things, despite the intuitive knowledge which told us that many of these teachings were false, later on we permitted ourselves to be almost hopelessly trapped. But that experience is for another chapter.

I had been studying Theosophy for about three years and had grown somewhat weary, not of the doctrines, but of the lack of spiritual incident, when I met one who has since become my teacher, or in Theosophical terminology, my Master: a friend and guide who has given me so much spiritual gold that the material wealth of millions could not suffice as repayment. Nevertheless, at the time when I met him he did not reveal himself as being an adept, nor did he do so until two more years had passed, during which period I was unconsciously being watched and tested.

Where I met him does not matter. It is sufficient to say that it was in the room of an organisation which has long since perished. In order to discuss some unimportant matters, a few people had gathered in a small room and we were waiting for him to arrive before commencing. As soon as he entered I felt an immediate difference in the mental atmosphere, which was enriched by the unseen largesse of peace, love and balance born from an impersonal personality. Up till then we had played with trivial topics of conversation, but shortly after he appeared our conversation rose, as though winged, from matters mundane to subjects mystical and occult.

I felt in a mysterious and subtle way that here was one who had delved more deeply than all others I had met. I felt as though the tangled and tall grasses of some Oriental jungle, growing over roads of great antiquity, were suddenly brushed aside; and the subtle current of attraction drew me to him, as the planet is drawn to the sun. The inner voice of intuition, powerful and compelling, that had so often spoken to me in the past and much more so in the last few years, told me in its forceful yet wordless manner that the knowledge I was seeking for so desperately dwelt within this man. Modest and aloof, he spoke of simple things in a low and gentle voice. But I sensed the golden realisations of spiritual things engraved within, and so I told him that I was greatly interested in matters occult. After the meeting was over, I asked him whether he would permit me to walk a little way with him; and though he told me little, I yet felt I would see him again; and, before we parted, he gave me his card and said that one day he would invite me to his home. So I left him, with great joy, but a little anxious, for I did not know how he looked upon me; often I would gaze at the card he had given me and longed to possess the courage to call upon him, though I fought against the temptation and waited.

A few weeks before meeting him, David and I decided to open a bookshop (an ambition common to literary aspirants), and after a lengthy search found what we imagined to be suitable. So on meeting my new friend a fortnight later I told him what we had decided upon. I had also mentioned to David the fact that I had met one whom I believed possessed great occult knowledge, and in describing him David felt as I did and became very anxious to meet him. Shortly afterwards we met him quite unexpectedly one Saturday afternoon. I introduced David to him and, after a short walk, he departed, promising to visit our new shop and wishing us luck.

And now, though I shall speak of him as M. throughout the rest of this book, I did not know his name until two years later, when he told me to address him as such. Nor did we know positively that he was our true teacher until we had played with spiritual fire and, getting severely burned, turned to M. for healing. But of this I shall write later.

After we had opened our small bookshop, he visited us as promised, from time to time, speaking of spiritual things, solving many problems, and shedding a new light upon much that puzzled us. He would relate little incidents of his life which if published would sound like fairy-tales. But it was not alone in conversation that he helped us. In order to show that what he spoke about was scientific, he would give us little demonstrations, simply and calmly, dispensing with all the paraphernalia generally used when a person claims occult powers. He never asked us to join any society nor to do the things of an eccentric nature that so many members of occult societies are asked to do; neither did he dress himself up in a cloak and bear himself as a man of mystery. He was human; interesting, and with a sense of humour. It was only in his conversations and demonstrations of certain supernormal faculties that he became as one apart. It was only sensitive people or those who possessed a certain understanding of spiritual things who would perceive the difference in atmosphere. He did not tell us to become vegetarians, nor were we prevented from smoking, nor from indulging in the many pleasures that young people love.

I think it was our motive that counted most with

M. Sincerity and a genuine desire to help humanity, coupled with the wish to understand ourselves, appealed to him. He would often say "Learn from everybody; listen to the child and the sage, for they may have something to teach you." He never sneered at the schools that claimed a complete knowledge of the mysteries. "If you wish to write to them, do so," he once said when I showed him an advertisement of a school of occultism. I discovered later that he knew they were charlatans, but he did not tell me so, preferring to allow me to learn from experience, as I was free to choose.

"Above all things, the soul wants three things," he repeated: "FREEDOM, LOVE, CREATION; and particularly creation, for the soul is most happy with that." And once having heard him speak about the Masters, I asked him if he would define their state of consciousness, and as an answer he brought me a book and there I found the definition:

A Master is an evolved being who has perfected a mental body in which he can function consciously while out of his physical vehicle. A Master, through that degree of Divine Force which his rapidly evolving Solar Body enables him to contact, has power to understand and to apply many of the laws governing the so-called phenomena of Nature. (Villars, *Comte de Gabalis*, p. 297)

Further it goes on to say:

Dante Alighieri makes mention of his first meeting with his Master with these words: "For there appeared in my room a mist of the colour of fire, within the which I discerned the figure of a lord of terrible aspect to such as should gaze upon him, but who seemed therewithal to rejoice inwardly that it was a marvel to see. Speaking, he said many things, among which I could understand but a few, and of these this: Ego dominus tuus (I am thy Master)." (ibid.)

M. told me that the book he lent me held a great deal of truth, and the commentaries had evidently been written by one who had had certain illuminations. The book told of other incidents, wherein certain men had met their Masters, and M. told me of cases occurring even in these days. He said that the Master might be waiting round the corner or even living in the same house in which the seeker dwelt, yet the Master would not reveal himself until the pupil was ready. And in turning back the leaves of the Book of Recollection, I can now read new meanings in what he then said, for he was our true teacher but could not tell us so until we had passed through certain trials, which certainly came very soon after. In these we more or less claimed that we had found a harbour for the ship of the soul, producing within ourselves feelings of pride and bubbles of arrogance that burst very quickly, leaving us all humbled and wiser.

Meanwhile, the visits of M. to our small shop produced a great joy, and we would listen eagerly to every word he uttered, drinking in a mental nectar that many seekers would give years of their lives to taste. Why we were so fortunate I can never understand, although it is true that we made great efforts to live according to our beliefs; but then so did many others. Neither were we too pure in our emotions. The explanation must lie in the fact that, as I stated before, we were sincere. From knowledge given I believe I may state that anybody who seeks earnestly and desires to become an instrument for the gods in helping humanity will probably meet if he persevere, as we met, after a number of years, a friend who would help him realise his ambitions. Naturally, failure often occurs, for the battle of the body against the soul is terrible, while the conquest of the mind is no easy task. Though I have learned a little, I yet know how exceedingly weak I am and often fear that the foundations I have endeavoured to build for so many years might crumble, and only through the help of God do I believe we can gain strength. When we possess the knowledge that the soul has a divine heritage; when we know that this heritage can only be given the soul after we have driven into its cage the animal that treads within the white monastery of the heart; when, while the soul is at prayer, we have sensed this animal breathing hotly amid the cloisters and snarling against the deep tones of the organ, until the incense of aspiration is lost amid the fumes of its breath; when we have driven out this monster that has crawled into the library of the mind, and upon the golden tablets of knowledge has smeared its hate—then, and only then, can we set free the warm ecstasy of spiritual love and bathe the soul and mind in its rich waters; thus purifying and etherealising our elements, and thus become more sensitive to hear the voice of the ruler within, whom we could never have heard until we had cleansed the channels of the soul.

When we have accomplished these things, the clamour of the outside world dies and man's developed soul can then read with ease the truth of the inner beings of others. And also a greater tenderness grows within those souls who have been illumined, for they see the latent magnificence of man: the imperial imagination that lies sleeping within him and its possibilities when awakened; they see the soul sheeted in robes of fire. They see the links that makes man one with all things. When the student discovers his true powers, he can then harmonise all those conflicting elements within himself: the animal becomes the servant, the soul the musical instrument to transmute the harmonies of Nature, the mind the balancing machine to balance the desires and thoughts, the imagination the flask for the wine of the sovereign spirit that rules and guides its small world.

But it was not occult matters alone that M. spoke about. He also told us what our talents were. At that period I was weakly fumbling and striving to write. I had attempted, like all ink-obsessed aspirants, the most-difficult art of verse; and though I was inspired often and felt all that ecstatic glow derived from creative effort, these mental butterflies invariably were but beetles when shown in fatherly pride to all who were kind and tolerant enough to look upon them; usually they provoked laughter or compassion with gentle reminders that, "I also wrote verse when I was young." Why verse has always been looked upon as a form of adolescence I have never understood; probably rhyme being easy they imagined therefore that poetry was easy, when it is as difficult as any other form of art. Whenever I showed my efforts to M. he did not find them food for amusement, as so many others had done, but encouraged me in my attempts, though I now know that the work of that period was pathetically bad. Yet M. encouraged me to practice an art that to an uncultured, ill-educated youth needed the utmost refinement. Although I afterwards met a girl who developed my technique, it was M. alone who evidently saw within me something

I did not dream I possessed. It is true that ever since I was a child the pen held a fascination for me, but how M. knew that I could write verse when I only expected to write prose has always puzzled me.

The eventual result of my writing was that I turned the shop into a studio; and though I never neglected a customer, I would be considerably annoyed if interrupted in the midst of a poetic spasm, for I would spend hours sitting at the counter, meditating on a rich, luscious line and licking with my mental tongue the flavour of a beautiful, pulsating word, chanting it softly until I was intoxicated and saw the customers lost in a distant warm haze, while the faint name of some cheap and popular novelist floated up to me. No, I was a decidedly incompetent bookseller, for who would sell books when seated on a throne of fire; who would care for pence when lost amid the dreams of hashish; who would want to answer mild old women when captaining the myriad legions of the stars. And even when I left the turrets of the heavens and folded my mental wings, I would argue with shifty-eyed Bohemians and youthful egoists who made our shop their home, arguing until the fire of anger seized me (instead of the fire of inspiration), heating me to a boiling-point that would overflow against those who had the temerity to disbelieve what I said. And yet the shop existed and we sold sufficient to pay our rent, while David roamed about London for bargains.

But despite our efforts few customers really came, for the shop was situated in what one could call a consumptive street, where many other shops seemed to be dying by degrees, until we realised we had practically pitched our hopes upon a Saharan spot. It was one of those streets that are forgotten through being like a courteous old gentleman, who has lived on in an ill-mannered and bustling generation. We chose this street for many reasons; one the artistic—we argued that people preferred buying books from an old-fashioned and pleasant shop, for I think books need courtesy and consideration, an unruffled and gentle atmosphere, not a new and brightly polished home, nor a grimy and dusty home where the stale smell reminds one of a rag-picker's shop. Had we succeeded, we might have developed that mellow and unhasting atmosphere. Unfortunately, we only rented half the shop, the other side belonging to a person who *could not* have contributed to our ideal. The second reason why we wanted that place was because it was not too dear; and thirdly it was in Bloomsbury, which we knew was a students' district, but unfortunately they never discovered our existence. I still think that had we opened our shop in a busier district we might have made a success, for we did understand the value of books; but starting with small capital and great ideals in the wrong spot was fated to produce failure. The mist of ideals is generally blown away by the breath of the giant Business, and for these reasons we existed only about six months, wherein our dreams of success melted rapidly into the bleak and flint-like rocks of common sense against which we stubbed our toes often and painfully. For we mistook our weakness for kindness, and our impracticality as proof of being finer clay; we used the shop as a salon and studio, and so mostly attracted the bohemian, who was naturally penniless.

Meanwhile the frequent visits of M., who would visit us late at night, dissolved all our little dissatisfactions and anxieties. He often told us to be business-like, but we were so young and brimming over with dreams, wishing to use the haze of ideals in order to smooth the rough edges of the world, that we took little notice of such advice, though any occult knowledge given would be eagerly taken to heart.

It is difficult to recall all he said, but what I remember I shall put down in the course of the book. Many things were of a fantastic nature, occult experiences and adventures that would not be believed if I mentioned them, though I have not the slightest reason to think them untrue. He told us many things about ourselves which we did not believe anybody else could have known for they were private. He would give us clear descriptions of people unknown to him but whom we personally knew, their habits, talents, etc.; but all the small demonstrations were but little things he told us, for there were many things which could not be shown to us as we were not ready, and moreover there were more important things than magical demonstrations. We should have to practice certain mental and physical exercises and endeavour to attain a certain balance before knowledge and power could be given to us. For to place explosives in the hand of a child is not alone dangerous for the child but also for the person responsible; such is the occult law, the master being responsible for his pupils. Another aspect is the satisfying of people's curiosity, and once I asked M. about this. He told me the story of an adept who wished to boast of his accomplishments in the presence of a company of people, so he materialised a certain food only to be found in a distant country; but after he had done so his power was taken away. This same adept once threw out of his window in sheer extravagance a sum of money, for he was exceedingly wealthy. The result was that he died a poor and blind man; for the money had been given to him for spiritual purposes. He had acted contrary to the spiritual law, for being an initiate he possessed greater knowledge than the normal man; and knowing, as M. said, that money after Wisdom is the second power of this world, he had to suffer much more severely than those lacking the spiritual illumination. The Higher Self, M. said, is very stern, and particularly so when the body has passed through certain initiations. The first law was to use your common sense.

Another subject on which I questioned M. was about the elementals, for he often told little stories about them. They comprised the gnomes, representing earth; the undines, representing the soul of water; the sylphs, whose region was the air; and the salamanders, spirits of fire. Before relating some of these tales, I shall write down from this strange book that M. brought me a definition of these Nature elementals.

Man's consciousness [this book says] is limited in direct proportion to the development of his senses of perception. Man has within himself, in the sympathetic and cerebrospinal nervous systems, minor brain centres. When by purity of thought and life and the right use of Solar Force,* man awakens and energises these centres, he is able to penetrate into other states of being and discovers himself to be living in a

* "Solar Force 'is the Paraclete, the light of the Logos, which in energising becomes what may be described as living, conscious electricity of incredible voltage and hardly comparable to that form of electricity known to the physicist' (Pryse, *Restored New Testament*, p. 8). THIS FORCE CAN BE GOVERNED BY MAN, AND WHEN GOVERNED IS THE INSTRUMENT WHICH THE SOUL USES TO BUILD UP MAN'S SOLAR OR SPIRITUAL BODY," (Villars, *Comte de Gabalis*, p. 48)

world teeming with intelligences and entities existing in certain well-defined realms of consciousness hitherto unknown and unperceived by him.

Paracelsus sheds light upon the method whereby man may make acquaintance with the Peoples of the Elements when he says, "We come to the conclusion, then, that all the Elements are not joined together, but that they are altogether aerial, or igneous, or terrestrial, or aqueous, solely and without admixture. This, also, is settled that every Element nourishes itself, or does that which is in it or its world" (*Hermetic and Alchemical Writings*, vol. 2, p. 271). For when those centres in man which are intimately related to the distribution of the essences which nourish the Earth, Air, Water and Fire Bodies, or vestures of man's spirit, have been regenerated, man is enabled to attain ranges of consciousness coextensive with those of the four races of beings inhabiting the essences of these four Elements, since the Peoples of the Air, "the Dwellers in the Earth, the Nymphs, the Undines and the Salamanders receive their lifelong bodies in an alien essence" (ibid., p. 340). Their bodies are built up of those finer materials which interpenetrate gross matter and its interspaces, even as man's own finer bodies are thus built up.

When speaking of the four Elements, their range of vibration in matter is meant. Obviously visible and transitory flame cannot be the habitat of a long-lived race. Yet the Element of Fire, or its rate of vibration, interpenetrates every manifestation of Nature, even the grossest, as the finding of radium in pitchblende evidences, and in this clearly defined range of vibration a race of intelligences highly differentiated and evolved has its being. The essences of the Earth, Air and Water are also filled with conscious and appropriate life. If man will purify his body, emotions and mind he may, through knowledge of the Law governing the Solar Force and the regeneration of certain minor brain centres, enter into a harmonious relationship with these People of the Elements. (Villars, *Comte de Gabalis*, pp. 30–32)

Although I am aware that to the man of science the above quotation may sound absurd, for science teaches us not to accept that which the *majority* cannot see or demonstrate, I yet speak of these matters because I know that science continually discovers to be true what it was positive were but the wild guesses of the ancient philosophers and mystics. We know that the rock of materialism is fast changing into a jelly; loose, quivering and soft. The lumber-room of man's mind is dark and cobwebbed, and but a few feeble rays can peer through, while in all the corners piled high are the mental bones, picked from the museums of the past; meatless, dry and brittle; upon a table as though upon a throne is a skull, molded and brought to birth by the materialist of the past, a bloodless and lifeless thing since its inception. Those eyeless sockets have never seen, and the mouth has never spoken, for only the head was formed; they could not complete and fix to the skull the limbs or flesh or heart, for they did not adventure into the deeper realms of the soul. Their minds strove to photograph accurately, but the other instrument—intuition—was asleep. How much more philosophic is the savage, who, with the mind of a child, and maybe because he is a child, and lacking the scales of thought, seeks in his crude and strange manner the underlying cause of a disease by attacking evil spirits and powers he cannot see, yet intuitively knows to exist, compared to the materialist who limits himself only to the inaccurate vision of the eye or the instrument. It is only recently that he has accepted the fact that mind plays an important part in the health of a person; who knows but soon he will find that he may possibly cure many diseases without the aid of serums, though he has not yet mapped out the anatomy of the emotions, believing them to be one and the same with the mind. Perhaps a few years more and we shall be compelled to accept many more beliefs of the occultists that are now ignored or treated with contempt. For the occultist, being more sensitive through certain developed subtler senses, has a greater knowledge and understanding of hidden things and motives of people than the most sensitive instrument of science could translate. The occultist and mystic feels the suffering of humanity as one would feel the scalding of boiling water.

M. has often told me what an agony it is sometimes to mingle with people who send out waves of passion and hate; and though personally I have been a student only for a short time, yet through the practice of my exercises I can feel the emotions, mental feelings and states as positively as one would feel if struck on the physical body. I have discovered that the emotions sent out by people differ in degrees, according to the strength of their passions. And I realise how much more so must M. feel the atmosphere of unpleasant people, for the senses grow finer and finer until one feels not alone the passion of one but the passions of many; not alone when they are near but also when they are at a distance.

As the senses become more and more ethereal so must one ultimately become as one apart, and though he may dwell alone he yet feels the sufferings and loves of people as when he dwelt with them. But just as he receives impressions so can he return impressions and send help to people from a distance.

The scientist has proved chemically the unity of things; the occultist has proved it emotionally and mentally. Feelings flow against him as the waves of a sea, yet as a tower of steel veined with gold he stands motionless and calm; he dare not give way, otherwise he would be invaded by powers that would do him much harm because of his greater capacity for suffering than the normal person possesses.

Yet those worshippers of the skull of scepticism that leers upon them with lipless mouth smile in vague amusement upon the mystic with his belief in God, upon the child for its imagination, upon the savage for his ignorance. "Why," they say, "have we not had the experiences that you have had; we have not had visions; we have not had premonitions, the custodians of the future have not told us what is to be?" In the same manner they can say to the botanist, "We walked the field you walked in, yet we did not see the rare plant you gathered"; or to the gold-seeker who found gold, "We did not find gold though we travelled over the same land." When the sceptic enters the laboratory of his soul and experiments with the mental and moral elements he will find there, then after a certain time he also will get results; just as there have been pioneers in the realm of science, so have there been pioneers in the realm of the soul. And here I again will state certain things M. told me in regard to the existence of wiser men than those of the West. I once asked M. if he could tell me something about symbols and he pointed to a young doe with a piece of fungus in its mouth which enriched a lacquer cabinet; he mentioned that to the initiate there exists in the world today an aristocracy of intelligence into whose mental sphere few Western minds had been able to penetrate; to these initiates the symbol of the doe and fungus represents the wisdom that would come to an old man when he will place his mind in the attitude of a child to receive instruction from conscious nature, i.e. the elements of earth, air, fire and water. To the Westerner this symbol merely represents long life.

"Do you realise," M. continued, "that when the Western peoples were living in caves, gnawing bones and painting their skins, this civilisation was living in brick houses, sitting on well-designed furniture and clad in silk? And today if you wish to contact this consciousness of intellect, you must extend the range of your mental atmosphere, scientific and filled with knowledge as it is, to harmonise with that of this older race, otherwise they will be a closed book to the seeker.

"Of this intellectual caste a wise man once said to me, 'Why do you spend so much time in giving help and knowledge to that man of lower caste,' and I replied, 'Should not a man through sacrifice labour to serve those below him.' Quick was the response, 'In helping those below you, you are sometimes dragged to their level and then their conditions hinder you from asserting your own true sovereignty of Nature on your own plane.'" And M. asked me who was the wiser one. Whilst I was puzzling over the question, he said, "Often through guidance of the heart and not through wisdom we inflict burdens not alone upon ourselves but upon others; therefore work not for the individual but seek to establish a better relationship between man and man *in the mass.*"

Modern science has made many useful discoveries, but it needs to learn much more from those whom it ignores and treats with contempt. It is unfortunate that the Westerner lacks the subtlety of mind which the Oriental possesses. The soul pioneers have experimented for thousands of years, and who knows all they have discovered: is it likely that they would persist in that which produced no results? Have the Westerners ever produced such magnificent religions, full of subtlety, logic, wisdom, psychology and hygienic training? Surely, if certain truths had not been discovered, these religions would have died for lack of food; as a hollow shell will, when struck by a hammer, crumble, so would have crumbled these experiments.

After all, modern science is aged but a few centuries, while our Ancient Science is thousands of years old; therefore it is grey-headed Wisdom who should smile upon vigorous baby Science. Maybe the far past also had some knowledge of science as nowadays controls the world, for I believe it is said that some ancient people possessed models of aeroplanes thousands of years ago. Who knows but that in some centuries to come we shall pass the need for flight in the manner known today, as we slowly discover the locked-up powers of Nature?

Nowadays Science has discovered forces that it generally uses for destructive purposes, just as a child destroys its toys through not having developed sufficient wisdom or balance to treat them rightly. We are so busy discovering things of an outside nature that we have no time to listen to the inner wisdom that is dwelling within us. Nowadays we crouch beneath the shadowy arches of incident, for the balm of Wisdom has not been sought, whilst our minds hop like sparrows picking up crumbs. We listen to the voices of our shouting moods and our impressions of life are slowly woven into a disharmonious pattern, like the flaring colours of a madman's dream; and scarcely a moment is given for meditation in the quiet temple of the spirit wherein can be found peace. Desperately we brood upon our small griefs and admire the sharpness of their weak thorns. Man has lost his youth, no longer the dancing child who is untroubled by time and who suck from the passing hours all the sweet flavours and juices. He steps warily and fearfully into the boiling cauldron of the days, believing each companion to hold a dagger, his heart shrinking with suspicion from those who desire friendship, whilst his lips flow with words that have a false warmth. Hypnotised, he stares through the soft-ledged windows of the eyes upon ever-changing and ever more wonderful allurements that entice him away from the hidden beauty locked up within the deeps of his soul.

Occultism cries: "Come back, in that mantle of clay as in a mausoleum are sepulchred the glad secrets of the golden period, entangled and tethered amid the warm earth; imperial secrets more majestic than the dreams of angels; forces that have made men kings and brought them into communion with the elementals of Nature, giving them power to command obeisance from the waves and holding in leash the baying hounds of thunder and tempest; commanding the sentinel gnomes to reveal and yield their treasures for the building and enrichment of temple and palace. Where men were as shining flagons of flame, treading with firm stride the velvet-caparisoned firmament of Earth in artless and impersonal knowledge of the wholeness of things."

Woven from the ethereal matter and receptacles of the divine liquor of wisdom sent by the gods, they knew that all life should be given love and not death. The powers of the soul can be converted into moral and mental wealth; and man who has been cast from the many dies of environment and has been weighed in the scales of harmony, plucking from the ages those experiences that have helped to perfect and complete the mould of his own being, has spent the wealth the ages have given in mental and moral dissipation. Have the aeons toiled with all their elements, bringing him the powers of thought and of feeling, the machinery and wonder of eye and heart—those windows of the material and the spirit—in order that he should destroy all that has been garnered within him for some divine purpose? We feel that if only scientists attempted to investigate these many claims that Occultism makes, they would understand the plan and purpose of existence.

The intuitions of the artists have discovered truths that only now are being accepted by science:

> All things by immortal power,
> Near or far,
> Hiddenly
> To each other linkèd are,
> That thou canst not stir a flower
> Without troubling of a star.
> > (Thompson, "Mistress of Vision,"
> > stanza 21, lines 5–9)

When William Blake saw "a World in a Grain of Sand" ("Auguries of Innocence," line 1), he saw with his intuition that which the scientist discovered after many years of painful research, though I admit that what he intuitively knew did little to advance the cause of science.

I have spoken at considerable length about the intolerance of Science, though I know that in the development of humanity it also has its important part to play; but only in order that greater tolerance would be shown by the sceptical to these little tales M. told me in regard to the elementals have I written these words.

One tale particularly M. was fond of relating. It was about a gnome who had been enchanted in the past by a magician to a certain book, giving this book a certain atmosphere. This gnome visited M. and asked him to disenchant him; and M. doing so, he became friendly and would often talk to M. and ask him questions. Once he said, "I know what you call night and day; it is the difference of vibration." At the time the great war took place it evoked hidden forces from the lower spheres, and those living in these spheres were greatly distressed at the turmoil above them; and this gnome asked, "Why is it we who do not destroy should be denied immortality?" M. explained to him that in time they would achieve immortality and that man himself in aeons past had also evolved from a similar element as the gnome—this particular doctrine is also Theosophic. M. also told me a number of other little tales which I have forgotten, but he told me that the gnomes are good friends to those who have lost valuables, but that one should never laugh at them as they take offence easily. Though I know what I relate will be accepted with much amusement, I write these tales because I know there are some who have probably had experience with the little people, for many people are clairvoyant enough to have seen them.

M. also often spoke to me about the sylphs, for whom

he had a great admiration, owing to their wonderful beauty and purity. The higher elementals will not permit the occultist into their sphere unless he is physically, emotionally and mentally pure, because the human body is offensive to them; also if the occultist desires to visit them he must obey their laws, for man, they say, is a destructive creature. They have, I was told, great knowledge in the manipulation of mind stuff and can help the magician, but will not help those who are destructive. Once a sylph of wonderful beauty visited M., and one thing M. noticed was her magnificent head of hair, which he believed had taken many days to fashion; and, he added, "Would take a painter a month to draw." He said he believed that many mystics who had been illuminated and saw a sylph imagined that they had seen Christ, so beautiful were these sylphs. One of them once said to M: "Do you not realise that we also have teachers who visit us, and that God is never apart from His creation?"

Though we had known M. many months, he had never spoken to us about the various, little food-fads that we practiced. As I mentioned before I had become a vegetarian and was a non-smoker and teetotaller like many members of the Theosophical Society; David being much more strict than myself. But we always forgot to question M. about these methods of health and sentiment that we imagined would help us to tread the Path leading to truth and initiation; in fact we took these things for granted in M.'s case, for we could not perceive one who was spiritual doing these things. But we were destined to be awakened, when one evening M. invited us to dinner at his home. On arriving David and I sat down willingly and hungrily, and to our horror and consternation found in the first course pieces of meat. We looked at one another and at M. in amazement; and he also gazed at us in surprise, for evidently he had taken for granted the fact that we ate meat. My surprise was all the greater because as I have mentioned elsewhere I have never met one with so pure an atmosphere, and the Theosophical Society had many vegetarians. So I asked M. the reason why he was not a vegetarian (though later on he told me that he ate very little meat really) and he gave me a number, one being that in England the people did not know how to make proper vegetarian dishes as they did on the Continent and in Eastern countries; also that the atmosphere of a great city to a very sensitive person is productive of much pain, particularly when attempting to live the Yogi life. Another reason was that in a land of meat eaters one would cause much embarrassment when visiting people and desiring special dishes; and, he added, the real occultist should never make other people feel uncomfortable; lastly as a final thread to the web of argument, the Tibetans who dwell in the centre of spiritual Buddhism eat sheep. Still, he continued, the fact that we had been vegetarians did us little harm and was good training in control because there would come a time, if we endeavoured to live the life of an occultist, when we would have to become hermits and practice all the asceticisms.

So from that evening onward, David and myself returned again to the fleshpots; and, speaking truthfully, not in great sorrow, for many vegetarians we had known were not, physically, very healthy.

Another thing we questioned M. about was marriage, whether it was unwise for a student to marry; and I understood him to say that the student was perfectly free to do what he would, though it would be inadvisable to marry a person who was below him in caste and development, for then he would more often be hindered than helped, particularly if he married when young. Though, of course, sometimes marriage could also help, for the student seeks balance; and if the student arrives at that stage, there is little to fear. And M. mentioned a case of a married Master with a family, whose wife was completely ignorant of the fact that her husband was different from the ordinary type of mankind, save for the exception that he possessed a vast knowledge that surprised his family.

Another question I asked M. was about failures; and he told me that many of his pupils had failed through sex, egotism and jealousy. "But," he added, "though they had failed they were not forgotten, and a time would come when the fallen pupil would be given another opportunity, for the Teachers are very patient and can understand the weaknesses of mankind because they had also suffered in the past before succeeding; treading the Path is a case of constant effort and, though years may pass, persistence in carrying out the various exercises will ultimately be rewarded with success, for not the smallest effort is wasted; and a moment comes when something is opened, some sleeping force awakened, and the seeker has a new realisation of life, an extension of the senses that makes one more sensitive of things that passed unnoticed before. Furthermore, sometimes our seeming failure and plunge into more material conditions are only apparent and lead, later on, probably to a swifter and fuller realisation of the truths of God than those who make few false steps and rise steadily higher. I am reminded of a student, more mystical and sensitive than myself, who had had spiritual experiences when very young. This student became so unpractical that his Higher Self plunged him through a series of experiences that brought him into contact with some of the coarsest and most materialistic of people, forcing him to see the world in a less rosy light.

And M. told me that those experiences would carry him much higher than those who had not been plunged into such a wide range of life; though also, he continued, it is really preferable to mount slowly and surely than rise like a rocket and from the heights descend ingloriously.

A few weeks after Christmas our shop began to pine through lack of nourishment. The few streams of customers dried up and we began to sense a coming calamity. Our vision of a large establishment, a large income, and a large amount of leisure began to recede to an impossible distance, and we realised that we could pay our expenses no longer. Therefore we agreed to cut our losses by seeking a cheaper place, and that idea was immediately carried out.

About a week before we moved I became acquainted with a girl named Estella, whom I met at a Theosophical lodge, and who was greatly interested in the various teachings of Theosophy and Bohemianism. She wished to meet strange people and have strange adventures. These I promised her, and they came sooner than I expected, for at the same time I came in contact with a new teacher upon the Divine Mysteries. Such indeed was the title, a grandiose habit false teachers generally have. David brought the advertisement to my notice, and as he seemed eager to attend these lectures; and also being somewhat weary of the Theosophical Society, I agreed to accompany him. So before writing about my adventures in our new home, I shall describe this new teacher.

HUMAN SPECTRA

Ponderers peering through the mist, builders of minarets of sand, ghosts who walk and laugh and work. You are bewitched by the shadows, the thoughts, the dreams of the hidden people. They are in your room, holding in their hands the secrets that would make you as gods. They overshadow you with their shekhinahs; invisible, they whisper to you, and you become inspired. They call themselves the humble servants of God, and you call yourselves masters of Earth. And yet you are as spectrums, reflecting their thoughts, their emotions, but diverting their shafts of power often for evil motives and flooding the Earth with stained beams of thought that return to the instrument, bringing with them destruction. Yet in the aegis of their love and their divine patience they still guide you into fresh realms of experience.

CHAPTER FIVE

THE FALSE PROPHET

Having read too much and realised too little while dwelling in the cosy nest of the Theosophical Society, we preened and unfolded our newly fledged wings and, with great uncertainty, flew into the hands of the bird-catcher who waited outside, ready to cage and pluck his unfortunate prisoners, and, incidentally, willing to teach his captives songs of his own composition. The which, on being captured, we did willingly and joyfully, but we were extremely bedraggled creatures that modestly and silently left his cage when we had learnt all his tunes.

S., for so I shall call him, was a man who had studied the psychology of sparrows. He knew what crumbs to scatter. He told us it was from the bread of faith, but he knew that the wheat had been grown in the fields of foolishness and mixed with the yeast of egotism. He also knew what melodies attracted us, frank and cheeky melodies with a touch of the daredevil in them, which later on we imitated perfectly and piped in fun content. But also he knew what whip to use; the whip of fear. For he would tell us often of the terrible birds of prey that flew outside our cage; the wicked eagles of the devil —his devil was a theatrical one, complete with hoofs, tail and horns, and holding, I believe, a large toasting-fork. It was a grinning devil that ruled the whole world and was preparing for the great moment when it could snatch the harps from the angels' hands—for his Heaven was also typical—and reign in evil sovereignty over the whole world. And also he told us that if we refused his protection we would be plunged into the darkest depths of Hell with all the other wicked creatures that infested the earth. So fear, faith and foolishness bound us to him as strongly as steel chains.

S. was old, with sparse grey hair; above medium height; and with the face of a hard business man and an eye quickly and almost magnetically attracted to a pretty ankle or face. For I recollect whenever he came to lecture us his eyes would sweep round the room, rapidly and surely, noticing the absence of some attractive women at once, and for whom he would inquire, welcoming them gladly if they appeared; usually asking them if they would like to visit his flat for the purpose of having tea and a heart-to-heart talk, and, if they were willing, a lip to lip.

How many couples he has parted we do not know, but of some we do; usually his disciples would leave their wives in order to follow him. Like David, Paul and myself, they were sincere but badly educated. This, David and myself noticed speedily, for having belonged to the Theosophical Society, where many members possessed a certain culture and refinement, we quickly observed the lack of it among our new acquaintances.

The lectures that S. delivered were undoubtedly interesting and vigorous, though often fragrant with an inspiration that certainly flowed from a source other than the spirit. Yet also often enough he was truly inspired; for he was a curious mixture of good and evil, though usually the beast guided the reins, making him cruel, lustful and thoughtless; an excellent study for those who have faith without thought, for those who will not learn that man is the mould of his thought, and that the actions of S. expressed the true man. He was extravagant, while many of his disciples were half-starved in order to pay for his comforts; while his uncontrolled passions contradicted his teachings of purity and selflessness; and his certain touches of cruelty for which there was no necessity proved his lack of divine love, about which he spoke often and lengthily. And this was the man whose music attracted us.

It is only now that we realise the full significance of our past actions, that we who were students and seekers had to choose between two paths: the path which led to light and the path that led to darkness; but at that time we did not understand the test through which we were passing. M., who watched and understood all that was happening, could say little. We had to make the choice; we had to learn and understand that would-be disciples must gather certain experience; we had to listen to the spiritual voice within us and obey it, or else be deaf to it. We were deaf, though we felt great trepidation and uncertainty. There was much twittering and shaking before we spread our wings. Who knows but that the voice of intuition spoke to us by making us feel uneasy? Nevertheless, S. gathered us into his aviary.

Eagerly thinking we had struck spiritual oil, through the wording of his advertisement, we attended his lectures. Our first impression was very disappointing, for he did not look at all like an initiate, but his opening words were certainly original and frank, for he called us a lot of fools and said that we were exceedingly ignorant, which was certainly true. And though we were startled we were also pleased. Here was somebody original.

Theosophic lecturers were generally polite and pleasant, but here was somebody who did not care whether he pleased his audience or not. The next thing he did was to call upon the platform a disciple, who had gone through all the initiations of S.'s divine mysteries, and poke fun at him, which the disciple listened to in a sheepish and naughty-boy–found-out attitude; and I think he deserved it, for if he had been so many years a member of S.'s school and had not sufficient faith in God to leave it, then all the jeers and sneers of S. were well-merited. But at that time we did not know the truth, so we smiled and thought S. very humorous.

It is worth mentioning here, in view of our later discovery of S.'s hypnotic influence, that on entering the lecture-hall, David was greatly impressed with the fact that the place was strongly permeated with some psychic influence. But whether it was spiritual or not, his lack of training made it unable for him to comprehend.

The lecture over, we hurried away, and for the next few days spoke of S. to everybody we thought likely to be interested. And I asked Estella if she would like to accompany me to hear a new teacher who had a wonderful message to man. She agreed, and we also persuaded the Irishman to do so; and thus the four of us attended the second lecture, which was a continuation of the first. The Irishman said little at the conclusion, but I believe he did a considerable amount of thinking—incidentally he was one of those in the Group who did not join the school—Estella also said very little. But David and myself began to believe that here was a new apostle of God, although we were extremely puzzled over many things connected with his personality and doctrine. Also his Christian terminology did not please us, for we were more used to Sanskrit terms when spiritual states were defined. He prophesied the end of the world, and at that period we had never met a teacher who said that, though many Theosophists expected the appearance of some great Being, and therefore his teachings held something new for us; though since then we have heard of many who prophesy the same calamity. Unfortunately, the dates conflict, and as each prophet is certain that God has chosen him alone to be His sole instrument, and they make positive statements in public to that effect, things become unpleasant when the skies do not rain fire and the Earth does not open her many mouths. And I asked M. if he could give me a reason for these prophecies and received this interesting answer. Many of these preachers are clairaudient and have heard voices by spirits, for the manifestation of great changes has caused people to expect greater changes still, which I think is most certain; so these self-styled prophets inspired with a certain knowledge and power make positive assertions, S. we believe being one of these prophets.

But David and myself had not heard of these things before, except in a vague way by astrologers, who state that the Earth is moving into another sign of the Zodiac, and in doing so will produce new influences in the minds and manners of man. So S. had said something really new; forgetting that virgin land to us may be very well trodden land to others, we eagerly adopted these new beliefs.

The hall in which we gathered was fairly large but was scantily attended, despite the grandiloquent titles of lectures advertised; and from further knowledge received through people about S., many really knew what he really was and warned us of the man. But we refused to listen and believed they were his enemies because of his teachings, and also that they were the unconscious instruments of the evil powers who attacked S., and about whom he constantly reminded us, because of the great message he had for man.

When addressing him, we called him Master, on the suggestion of one of his disciples, for they all addressed him as such, a title that in the light of later knowledge was absurd and totally incorrect; but we did as suggested, for we were ignorant and did not understand that a true spiritual teacher will not permit his pupils to call him "master," but "teacher." And here I will write down some things M. told me later.

There is no autocrat among a group of pupils, for each teacher is somewhat of a specialist along certain given lines; also it can happen sometimes that the apparently lesser-evolved member may become the teacher to the rest of the group, though even then he would not attempt to command or force obedience from the rest, for the freedom of each student is considered sacred, though all are supposed to work in perfect harmony for the good of all and for the good of mankind.

One of the saddest moments in a teacher's life [he continued] is when he is challenged by his pupil for knowledge, for the pupil's soul must be given freedom of expression, and anything that tends to limit the soul's expression brings upon the teacher the karmic responsibility.

This means that anyone who attempts to assist a soul in distress and is personal finds an opposition in the soul they wish to help. Therefore the teacher or priest who advises any soul about spiritual things should be impersonal and not desire to shackle the seeker in any way. But this was precisely what S. did.

A poet [M. quoted] has said: "Beauty, real beauty, ends where the intellectual expression begins" (Wilde, *Picture of Dorian Grey*, ch. 1), meaning that the intellectual generally produces personal feelings. Above all, let people alone with freedom for their soul's expression. The true student asks the other man's soul how he can help it, and the student's own soul will transmit the message. Keep the mind calm, for this is the higher form of clairvoyance, and the confessional, if done impersonally, is a spiritual thing.

It is noticeable that S., who called himself a Master, did not know any of these things in regard to the teachings of his pupils. M. had never told us to address him as master, and here I may state that the letter *M* does not stand for master, but another name. A teacher does not tell his pupil to do things; he may suggest and guide him as M. has done for us. Otherwise the pupil is perfectly free to act and do according to the dictates of his soul. Nevertheless, the teacher knows the secret thoughts and passions of his pupils, for he has linked himself to the consciousness of his disciples; and M. has told me that he has often used his occult powers in order to know how I am getting on, and often I have sensed his presence, for the teacher can visit the pupil in his mental body—but to this point I am devoting a complete chapter further on—or see clairvoyantly what he is doing. M. also told me about the waves of thought and emotion sent to him, and how he can distinguish which student or friend has done so, for each person possesses a different atmosphere, being also differently coloured; and as he is responsible for his pupils one can understand how carefully the teacher has to watch the one who desires to be chosen. Yet here was S., calling at the end of each lecture for pupils, accepting anybody who wished to belong to his school; there was no question asked as to the fitness of his would-be disciple, and evidently no thought or knowledge as to the responsibility he incurred. For his teachings spoke of initiations, a term that is much too lightly used when referring to the awakening of spiritual states of consciousness. But the other attraction that S. held out to us was the ease with which we could accomplish our pilgrimage. We could do what we pleased; we could indulge in all our animal desires, providing, according to S., we had Faith and Selflessness, and even the word *faith* meant to him that one should sit down and wait for the world to clothe us, feed us and pamper us. All this S. succeeded in doing admirably, when the true meaning of faith, M. told me, was "determinative energy."

We were also told by S.'s disciples not to notice or look askance upon any of his actions, as he was really what one could describe as a free-and-easy and cheerful sort of man, who sometimes became intoxicated, but otherwise was quite harmless. "Take no notice of my personality," he would say, and naturally we did not; but I think it was only because we did not yet know of his other vices which were not mentioned to us at all, and which we did not discover till later. Also some years before, we had met a Theosophic lecturer who had a similar disposition to S., though he did not make such preposterous claims, and being a Colonial of fresh virile character with a somewhat pagan outlook, though clean and straight in action, we foolishly imagined in our first meeting with S. that he was similar to the man we had previously met, except that S. possessed a much greater knowledge. And for those reasons we were prepared to listen to S. And here I will state M.'s answer when I asked him the reason for our adventure with S.:

The reason why the darker forces plunge the student into great ranges of experience and suffering is to produce balance, for the teacher seeks to place the student in the centre of the Path, advising him not to stray too far on either side.

And M., to whom we had spoken about our meeting with S., subtly warned us of S.'s hypnotic powers; but evidently we had to gain this experience. Therefore we listened to S.'s teachings, which though Theosophic and Gnostic in concept, yet had a different terminology.

S. had also written a number of books which were of great interest to us, and which we studied earnestly and continually. David sold all his occult library, and I did likewise, for we were told that these were no longer necessary, and that they were detrimental to our development. And so within a few weeks we were completely under the control of S. We neglected our business more and more and lived upon hope and faith for five months, leading a bohemian and half-hypnotised existence in our new quarters, about which I shall now write.

THE DARK HOUSE

Here, as in a dark house, man spends his moments; mourning the loss of the ancient lamps that once lit the rooms, those prophets and powers whose minds hovered calmly amid the curled-up thunders of God. Yet in the twilight porch these brethren gather and wait, listening for the deep chimes of the clock that will be the signal for them to enter and again bring light to the sombre chambers. They will open again the cob-webbed casements and light the hearth fires; they will again unseal the locked doors of the library and bring to man the old knowledge so long neglected, opening the yellow parchments and massive works stamped with the golden symbols of Truth. Soon the sonorous tones of the timepiece will ring so loudly that the echoes will vibrate in every room, awakening the heavy slumberers, who will leave attic and cellar, study and bedroom, and gather in the hall of the house; yet though hearing the footsteps of these brethren upon the porch they will not hasten to open the doors, but the bolts will move from their sockets without the help of hands, and the doors will open, letting in a swift gust of wind that will cleanse the whole building.

CHAPTER SIX
THE BASEMENT

At last freedom! Freedom from parental authority; freedom from the web of convention; freedom from the relentless pressure of enforced virtue; and freedom to listen to the whispering voices of Vice. And, greatest freedom of all, the luxury of laziness and initiation into the merry-hued realms of Bohemia, where we could earn the right to degenerate as speedily as possible and without hindrance. Freedom and love, starvation and cadging; and then the ultimate good hiding by stern Mother Nature for having leaped over the high walls of law, though naturally we knew nothing of the whipping to come.

With happy hearts we swiftly raised the flag of unconventionality and flaunted it in the face of every friend and acquaintance, calling all to our new home—the beggar, the unsuccessful artist, the completely deranged and the mildly deranged. "Come to our table," we said, "but bring your own food and some for us. We shall feast upon merriment, and our imagination shall transmute all the plain fare into rich and luscious foods. What matter the drab walls and discoloured ceilings, or the creaking stairs and disguised soap-boxes, for now we dwell in the illusive palace of pretence, where all pretenders shall be made welcome."

But it must not be imagined that we commenced housekeeping with such conceptions. Our degeneration started later. We really did attempt to continue our bookselling, and we succeeded inasmuch that we lived at least three months on our stock; the remaining period ending ingloriously.

Our new quarters were situated in a large, rambling basement in one of the squares of Bloomsbury; one of those strongly built and inartistic houses in which Bloomsbury abounds. This basement seemed to be permeated with an unwholesome and mildewed atmosphere. A vague and forbidding sense of evil appeared to ooze and drift within the dark rooms and staircase of the lower part of the house, and the only reason why we rented one of the rooms was for its cheapness, and that the tenant upstairs happened to be a mutual friend of ours; one who had founded a club in the upper floors, which later became disorganised through the gossip of members and the illness of the founder. Before the final disbandment of the club, many quarrels took place which resulted in considerable discomfort among ourselves. And here it is interesting to note one peculiarity about this place: that the subtle currents of these other people's moods seemed to strike one with positive and startling suddenness, as though by an invisible wave. I remember particularly one evening coming in after a peaceful and meditative walk, and descending the shadowy staircase, a sudden rush of violent anger struck against me, changing all my peaceful thoughts into an intense irritation against David, who happened to be in the room. It seems difficult to believe, but the sensation was so positive that I shall never forget the incident. The place apparently possessed a curious magnetic quality which I have never succeeded in defining. But these events, with many others, occurred later on, and when we moved in it was without qualms or uneasiness.

The room we occupied was very large and damp, with stone-flagged floor and dingy walls, whose plaster and paint crumbled into fine powder when touched. We made some fruitless attempts at cleaning and painting them but, with the exception of a wooden partition, failed miserably. This place had really been the kitchen of the house, for a huge stove whereon we could have cooked sufficient for a restaurant stood at the bottom of the room. Yet sombre as it all was, we made it more so by dividing it into two rooms with the aid of a huge pair of dark green curtains; one division in which we kept our stock of books and the other wherein we slept, ate and invited our friends. David slept on one side of our living quarters and I on the opposite side.

The shadows caused by the melancholy curtains were in perfect harmony with the subdued and depressing atmosphere and the dampness and darkness of the room. It was a study in grey and sad tones, and unfortunately we could not afford to buy any bright cloths or cushions. And truly for youth entering into the domains of Bohemia the portals were dismal enough, and now I can only conceive that our imagination and optimism must have been of a titanic order to view that place in a golden light, for the depressing influences touched us not at all.

Finally, being too poor to buy furniture, we were compelled to borrow from our friends things long ago discarded. David's treasure trove consisted of an old iron bed, an uncomfortable chair, and a sickly looking desk to be used in the shop. I arrived with two small, meek chairs, humble chairs that had been sat upon for so long a time that they wore a perpetual air of weariness and apology. Likewise I enriched our living apartment with a couch, black and filled with hollows whence the padding had slipped out, whilst the back was held in position by a large plank of wood. Our ingenuity in keeping the furniture from falling to pieces was considerably taxed; and a small table that had been nailed together hurriedly completed our home. The rest of the room held books. A primitive typewriter, bought on a foolish impulse, was the only sign of my serious intention to do literary work. Unfortunately the machine was broken by David about a week later, for in the ecstasy of seeing Rita enter he dropped it. This ended my literary aspirations for the time, though I doubt whether I could have written anything in such a place. For though I made many attempts, I constantly failed, and the only thing in which I did persevere was in falling in love. Furthermore, a host of friends, discovering our new quarters, were delighted with our free and easy methods of living and quickly made themselves at home.

But the most unpleasant incidents that occurred, from practically the first week of our residence, were the nightmares of David, and to this day we still believe the place was haunted. For we could hear footsteps at midnight (the conventional hour for ghosts) walking down the stone steps. And one evening when alone— David happened to be away that night—I heard the slow tread of somebody outside; and though I searched all the lower part of the house, looking in the wine vaults and all the other nooks and small rooms, I was relieved on being disappointed, for nobody was found.

Yet we have known other people who lived there after us, complaining about somebody who walked up and down the stairs at about three o'clock in the morning. An explanation is still to be found for David's nightmares, which would occur directly I extinguished the candles. As I mentioned before, we slept on opposite sides of the room, David on the iron bed and I on the couch. I was in the habit of reading late by candlelight, and all was well while the candle burnt. But immediately the light was extinguished, David would start out of his sleep and cry out: "Michael, quick! A light, a light. The Arabian, the Arabian!" And a stream of cold air would rush out upon me, coming from him like a blast of icy wind. After a few trembling attempts I would light the candles once again. David said that he saw a tall, dark man dressed in a long cloak moving towards him, and in all these nightmares it was always the same man. This apparition came to him constantly, though I confess I saw nothing. But of one thing we are positive, and that was the evil nature of the place.

I will relate the last proof of the existence of such a force and conclude that aspect of our quarters. A friend of mine rented a room there until quite recently. He was an inventor, and one of the most materialistic of men. Yet one evening he discovered the secret of rapid flight and a sudden belief in the existence of ghosts, for he swore he had seen and felt some one passing him on the staircase. It was, he said, like a thick, dark mist, silhouetted against a window, through which a cold, clear and full moon was shining. It passed slowly down the steps and through him, bringing with it all the sharp, icy thorns and chilling tendrils that climb and curl around the backbone when fear is bred. Unfortunately, my friend did not stay to investigate this phenomenon, though logically he should have done so; but like a number of scientific people when faced with supernormal phenomena, in which of course they do not believe, he made a most illogical and unscientific exit.

Thus in our new quarters we had all the elements of

an interesting and romantic existence: Bohemianism, love, mystical teachings by our new master; while in the background waited the patient and silent figure of our real teacher—and lastly, ghosts. What more could one desire, for we considered we had found peace and truth, love and freedom; and the truth really was that we were caught in the realm of illusion. In the Theosophic teachings the student is warned to avoid the realm of illusion. This we had imagined to mean that when one becomes an initiate he travels through a certain astral plane in which all things endeavour to attract him away from his real purpose; we had evidently forgotten that it was quite possible for the student to pass through the realm of illusion on this plane also, for that is evidently what happened.

My own love affair ended disastrously, though fortunately for the one who had infatuated me. I have previously mentioned something about Estella, who accompanied me to the lectures given by S. She was dark, good-looking, with black bobbed hair, a slim body of medium height, and carried a suggestion of hardness and practicality; yet withal a romantic strain and attraction to the weird and occult. She possessed a quick mental perception, though my clearest recollection of her was hardness and clear-sightedness, qualities much needed when moving about in our atmosphere. Her intelligent interest in the occult and quick perception of the subtler shades of meaning were the chief foundations upon which we built our friendship.

I flung myself whole-heartedly into a tempest of intense passion; how difficult it is to awaken again such a sweet and unbearable fire, that at that period burned through me. It seems now as if I had been swept through a river of flaming waters that sang lingering and lulling songs to me as I was driven on and flung suddenly and violently upon a bleak and desolate shore; yet such an adventure was good for me, and though this infatuation lasted only for three or four months it left my mind richer and riper for the experience. And I think the reason why I fell in love was through the glamour of the environment. David's girlfriend Rita was the direct opposite to Estella in appearance and temperament; fair, well built, comely, and much more intuitive than intellectual; therefore, from the aspect of light-hearted companionship, much more pleasant. I think too many intellectual and critical qualities are apt to mar the enjoyment of a company, though I could not say that about Estella, who did not awaken her critical powers when among us. I must admit that I possess a considerable amount of the critical quality, which often prevents the views of other people from being clearly expressed by its mental opposition, for it acts upon the mental body like a spear, stabbing the thought of people and thus producing dislike and disharmony.

A short while after we moved in our two friends, Paul and the Irishman, came to live with us. Paul's delightful and dangerous hobby of collecting strange souls from those unguarded asylums, the weird café's of Bohemia, was as strong as ever, and he would bring to our basement unkempt and outlandish loungers. Artistic tramps who unloaded upon us a delirious debris of useless visions, tattered fragments of rag filched from the robes of the muses and shown to us in pride. They were people half-suffocated by the fog of discoloured dreams, in which they would promptly surround us, leaving us gasping and spluttering mentally. We would listen intently and eagerly to these newly discovered and unrecognised geniuses, feeding upon their impossible ideals, but seldom being in the position to feed them with more material substance. It is significant that many of them were utter failures, though some had had good opportunities. Twisted mental vision had destroyed their sense of proportion, magnifying their small talents excessively, increasing their egotism and emotions, and altogether making them impossible to live with and unable to move among the sane people they sneered at and called Philistines. Also among them the well-secured mental breeches and petticoats of convention and society were too often considerably slackened.

Thus here in this dismal basement we would gather, evening after evening, wasting our time in futile discussion; the Irishman grumbling at women, whom he deemed the anathema of all creation, grumbling at the modern vices of life, and grumbling at things I cannot now remember; it is sufficient that he grumbled. Yet he possessed attributes of generosity and friendship for all his grumbling that were at least sincere, for he undoubtedly was, despite his criticisms, a sincere student of things spiritual, and maybe much of his irritability was caused through his being too sensitive. He would sit with legs outstretched upon another chair, puffing away at his small, black pipe, and telling us of his adventures in the various countries he had visited; or else reading passages from a little book he had carried in his pocket for years, entitled *The Bhagavad Gita*, and attempting to define its various mystical thoughts; or sometimes he would recite from Walt Whitman, whom he admired for his strength, praising the word cascades and then suddenly rising in an abrupt manner and leaving us, as though disgusted with the whole company because we did not get excited about the passages he so much admired. While Paul also talked, re-echoing the beliefs of the Irishman, and repeating the eventually annoying psalm, "All is illusion, all is illusion"; and sometimes changing it into the Sanskrit word, "All is Maya, all is Maya," which meant the same thing. Nevertheless he took a keener interest in everybody and everything than possibly we did. While David, wrapped in an Oriental calm, listened with evident relish to the Irishman's outbursts against women, though since then he has been the first of the group to marry; pale and more sensitive (though we were all sensitive, myself the least), he would sit silently. While I, similar in excitable temperament to Paul, would endeavour to argue, only to be instantly and relentlessly suppressed by the group, who still considered me one of the barbarians belonging to the normal race of the world, not being as unconventional as they desired, and therefore lacking those spiritual virtues that only the elect and unconventional possess.

An old-fashioned oil lamp placed upon a huge, badly stained cupboard we had found in the house (later on broken up for firewood by Paul, when he was given the occupation of caretaker by the landlord) illuminated with feeble beams our somewhat shabbily dressed gathering, who frequently drew up the couch to the great stove and attempted to warm themselves, for it was too large a room to heat by the small amount of coal we could afford to use. Only when Estella and Rita visited us were we alone; otherwise, aside from the Irishman and Paul, various minor acquaintances came. Estella would often bring in fruit for the party, and Rita some flowers to dissolve the depressing atmosphere with a little colour. Estella did not visit us as often as Rita, and I could see that she was greatly dissatisfied with our manner of living. Our future appeared so nebulous; we were spinning the foundations of our lives from the shadowy fabrics of vague ideas and beliefs; our thoughts for the future under the aegis of our newly discovered "Master," S., were no longer considered. I did no writing, though she often questioned me as to whether I had done any, encouraging me and waiting to see if I would take my literary work seriously.

But David and I were drifting. We never thought what would happen to us after we sold our fast-dwindling stock, for we did not think of the morrow, as S. continually told us to have faith and that God would always look after His own, that we should live upon the pinpoint of a moment; and though it was possibly true that God would look after us, we should not have accepted the fact as an opportunity for laziness. But unfortunately these teachings fitted in with our views of life. For we felt that we had reached a spiritual haven and security. Reading S.'s books, we found, like the old and fanatical students, portents and meanings in every small incident of the world, studying each page again and again, and finding a new meaning behind an old one. And really it was amazing how we managed to fit in the most trivial detail to harmonise with the general scheme of his philosophy. And here I must add, from that aspect they were well written, and of course as we speedily forgot our old ideas we were untroubled by a different scheme of life.

But we did not definitely join his school for a number of weeks, till one morning, when I awoke and on the impulse of the moment wrote to him, asking him to permit me to become one of his pupils. Previously we had investigated more deeply the teachings of other schools, as I have mentioned elsewhere; but one was too coldly intellectual, the other too narrow, another too broad; and so we decided that the real knowledge lay in the keeping of our new teacher. The same morning I wrote asking to be admitted, David did likewise, and furthermore we both agreed to write a letter to M. (who had not revealed himself to us as our true teacher) and state that we had arrived at our spiritual destination. We also definitely broke our ties with the Theosophical Society.

Then in our enthusiasm we endeavoured to sweep in a number of friends: Paul, Estella, Rita and the Irishman, and some new acquaintances. And we even asked M. if he would like to listen to one of S.'s lectures, and in reply M. visited us and said he would attend one lecture. Later on when we asked him why he did so, having realised how much more M. knew than S. regarding spiritual things, he told us that one should have the attitude of a child to all teachings that claim to be spiritual, for in that way one could learn from most unexpected sources; also he said that S. had made some spiritual contact but had also awakened an evil power, thus speaking many truths but acting in direct opposition to his teachings, indulging in the vices of a roué with all the women he met. Yet about this we had little knowledge, as the women naturally kept quiet, though they had discovered what the man was and to our great surprise avoided him. Only when he had practically hypnotised the wife of one of our friends, and her story made us aware of his hypnotic power, did we awaken to the truth.

Another thing he did was to accept from us all the money we could afford to give, though he knew how poverty-stricken we all were. True, it was but a few shillings, but it meant a great deal to us. Yet he accepted it all; and as we were pliable material, he had mentally hypnotised us to believe in all he did, without a word of protest. What mattered all our readings, studies and abstract philosophies when we did not have the spiritual eyesight to discern and understand the false from the true? We measured with our emotions and, lacking mental balance, became blind and bewildered. While standing and waiting patiently in the background was our real teacher; one who did not force us to give money for wisdom or join a society; one who did not preach down to us or bully us, who did not tell us his teachings were the only true teachings and all other false. Instead he calmly waited for us to learn our lesson, constantly repeating one sentence to us, the which we did not have sufficient discrimination to obey, that "above all things the soul wants is FREEDOM, LOVE and CREATION." The teachings of S. did not give us these things. Had we truly realised this saying we would have saved ourselves much mental pain later. But we were very young and impulsive. We wanted spiritual realisations without working hard for them, and S. promised all that.

So in our basement quarrels took place. Many were against S., and ourselves fanatically for him. I endeavoured to get Estella interested and begged her to join, and later on she did but left almost immediately. Many weeks before, she had definitely tired of me and stated so in a letter, and now on remembering all the time I wasted at that period I agree with all she did. For we were degenerating speedily, entangling ourselves in a network of uncontrolled sensuousness, whittling away all the little refinements that are part of civilisation in the loose atmosphere of Bohemianism. Nearly all our books were sold and David was already selling his private collection; while the people who visited us were of a much lower order of intelligence and culture, and filled the places of the finer members who had wearied of our society and of S., giving us therefore a clear field for our mental sowing and reaping.

And for all these reasons, including the one that she did not desire to float with a drifting vessel, Estella rejected my companionship.

When Estella wisely declined my worship in an unexpected letter, I felt that my martyrdom had commenced through belonging to the school of S. Sacrifices had to be made, and though melancholy persisted in haunting me, wailing and beckoning me to join the hosts of castaway lovers who in happy misery complain of their loss before her shrine, the pain was slightly dulled through my belief that I had taken the first step along the Path. Looking back now I can see that my vanity felt the pain much more than my heart, an aspect that happens often. And after all, why should we say to the one we love: "You belong to me?" It is only a desire of the flesh, a desire to gain power over a person's body and soul.

And no person has that right, only God. Love, I believe, is when a couple harmonise upon all planes, the physical, mental, emotional and spiritual; and that may be the reason why so few marriages are successful, for very few people can harmonise and love selflessly. And from further understanding I now perceive that I loved the melody of love, but not the player.

How much more dismal and gloomy the basement now appeared. The steady dripping of the watertap sounded as though it were weeping in sympathy, whilst passers-by walked with muffled tread. The furtive shadows on the wall nodded their heads as though in sorrow, and the shabby furniture looked shabbier still and creaked mournfully, and oh how hard and heavy and disorderly all things were; the houses were built the wrong way, the blue of the sky was too blue, the twilight was not dark enough, while the night was not black enough.

In the morning, chirruping birds sounded far, far away, like a distant plaintive memory, wakening me to the unbearable and weighty burden of another day; where before I shouted, I now whispered and trod tiptoe.

"The only thing," said David knowingly, "is to get drunk and so forget her. Today we shall buy some biscuits and cake and a bottle of wine. I have a few shillings and Rita will also contribute. Come shopping with us." So I walked behind them, a bowed and brooding figure refusing to be comforted and swallowing hard. Having made all the purchases, we returned to the dungeon that had evidently grown darker still in our absence and laid the table for the unaccustomed festival.

David poured out some wine and offered it to me.

"But why get drunk," I moaned. " She's gone," and I looked gloomily upon David, who joyfully drank the wine.

"Is it good wine?" I asked reproachfully, because I liked wine.

"Yes, it is excellent wine," they said, smacking their lips, and again offering a very small amount which I certainly refused. I enjoyed my suffering far more than all the wine in the world.

"Let's go for a walk," they suggested; and thoughtlessly added, "It's a nice evening."

I answered tearfully, "I don't want to go for a walk and it isn't a nice evening."

"Have some fruit," David suggested, and he offered me an apple, which I accepted but found quite tasteless. "I can't eat it," I sighed and looked sadly at the gap in the apple.

David then suggested we should go to the country for the weekend, as the Whitsun holidays had commenced. Meekly and dolefully I assented, and we agreed to leave London and camp out with two small tents, which we fortunately possessed, having used them in the previous year's holiday when we endeavoured to live the simple life somewhere in Devonshire. So starting early the next morning, David and I departed and ultimately arrived about twenty miles beyond London, where we pitched our tents. Still stunned with Estella's rejection, I walked as though in a state of hypnosis.

The first day waned into a mellow, moonlit and meditative evening, the kind of evening when the musician of time composes hushed and wistful themes for the souls of lovers; elusive and gentle moods that drift in silent waves into the flowering hearts of drowsy and love-quickened listeners. We were camping upon a public common beside a small lake, rush-fringed and shining silverly. While the voices of distant murmuring lovers drowsily rippled and approached my ears like the last echoes of a swan-song, but as each rhythm of the air caressed me they withered. There was too much quiet joy in the notes and I wanted to hear a sorrowful and grim tune, for I felt sure the composer of that evening played his delicious theme from a brutal and malicious desire to hurt me. David had long ago vanished into his tent, but I gazed at the unclouded, fat, grinning and self-satisfied moon, wondering why some dark and stormy clouds did not erase her smiling face from the heavens; and listening to the eddies of languid and sleepy sound in long-faced misery, until, brimming and overflowing with depression, I entered my tent and hunted Estella in my dreams.

After three woebegone days we returned homewards, to be met on opening the door by an eager and homesick dog that Paul had borrowed from somewhere and left in charge during our short absence, and who did not even trouble to welcome us but flew out of the door as rapidly as possible. I did not blame the dog; probably it was a well-brought-up dog, for on entering the room we discovered a badly littered and untidy floor; and while pondering over the strange mess, were greeted by Paul, who was bubbling over with the important news that he had met an entirely new group of unconventional people. That of course solved the meaning of the littered floor. Afterwards we discovered that these new friends were worse than all the preceding ones.

But now I determined to leave the basement; its gloomy and depressing atmosphere, the quarrels, the semi-starvation and the dampness. A week later I returned the broken couch, the two weary looking chairs and the clumsily made bookcase to the owners; and departed.

But I had not yet ended with the basement. David and Paul still lived there, though David was preparing to leave and marry Rita. Paul was permitted to remain through the kindness of our friend, the tenant of the upper floors, and become the caretaker of the whole house. This suited him admirably, as it gave him opportunities to help and give free lodgings to all the tramps he met in his nightly investigations of Bohemia. For Paul delighted in helping the downtrodden; unfortunately he made no attempt to discover whether they were deserving of his help or not. How many slept in the basement during his reign we do not know, but we met quite a number; for there was room for quite twenty without disturbing the rent-paying occupants. Unfortunately Paul's reign quickly came to an end through befriending two tramps, one of whom attacked Paul's employer, who had the temerity to insist that Paul do a certain task. This was too much to the indignation of Paul's companion, who considered that his benefactor was above menial labour and who stated so in forceful language. The result was that Paul, together with his companions, was immediately ejected.

About the same period, S., who was looking for a meeting place wherein he could deliver lectures to his disciples and dupes, rented through our recommendation a room overhead. How proud we felt. A real, genuine Master was working in the same building in which we once dwelt; and further still, more wonderful news with two other disciples of his who had become Masters under his tuition. We looked with awe upon these two men and approached them with due reverence and humility; pleased to be noticed by them; pleased to breathe the same air sent out by royal lungs; and pleased to sit beside them and listen to their kingly wisdom. Later on a very cruel trick was played upon one of these so-called Masters, giving us an insight into the character of S., and also the danger of carrying faith to absurd extremes. This Master was earning, after working very hard, a tolerable living. He was old and grey-haired, pleasant and gentle; and as a personality we liked him. S. told him to leave his occupation that he had developed with such labour and take up an occupation wherein even trained men had found it difficult to earn a livelihood. Why S. bid him do this we do not know, and when we were told the news, were greatly surprised and a little shocked at his command. Probably it pleased S.'s vanity to know that men had such faith in him.

Nevertheless we still clung to his teachings, passionately and hopefully. Whether he possessed a certain power or whether it was but imagination still puzzles us, but every time we listened to his lectures our eyes felt dazed and sleepy, as though an actual force emanated from him and hypnotised us. And later on this discovery resulted in our abandoning his control over us.

A certain friend of ours, whom we persuaded to join, brought his wife with him. A few days later she was found walking about in a daze. Her husband, sending for a doctor, was told after the examination that it seemed to be a case of hypnosis. Afterwards it transpired that S. had been interested in this woman and had evidently attempted to hypnotise her, for that is what she stated. Our friend, who had not appeared for a few weeks, visited us and told us the reason for his absence, namely, the startling incident about his wife, and suggested that S. was a fraud and an evil influence. I am only mentioning the first discovery we made. Afterwards many other things were told about him by those who had been unfortunate enough to come within his power.

The evening after this dénouement S. came to deliver his weekly lecture, and that evening I determined to fight this sleepy influence and see how S. reacted to it. I also told his chief disciple this news, but he replied that he disbelieved it. I retorted that if we were wrong in disbelieving in the genuineness of S., we had at least sincere motives, and that I did not believe that a sincere seeker had anything to fear. At the same time, S. had developed such a power over us that we actually feared the consequence of a revolt on our part against him; for we had been told that only the elect would be saved, and all the rest of the human race would perish in torment. An old conception that I believe many religions in the past have had. But these teachings were new to us in relation to our old Theosophical studies. And I had often worried over the fact that the teachings of S. were only printed in English.

What would become of the non-English races? Were they to perish because they did not know the English language?

It was in great fear that we determined to face him, and when he began to speak I gazed steadily and continually at him. Watching him keenly, I felt that he sensed our anger; and I thought if he was not the hypocrite we believed him to be, he would be able to smooth and explain matters, where explanation was necessary. But we could see that he was uneasy, for his lecture rapidly became farcical. He could not face us and stammered and clutched at his words as though mentally drowning. Very soon he stopped the lecture and dismissed the meeting, and that was the conclusion of his Mastership. He left London immediately without any explanation, and we sent him a letter suggesting that he should stay away permanently. This he acknowledged and, as further proof of our discovery of him, agreed to remain away.

Like sleepwalkers suddenly awakened and considerably humbled we gazed sheepishly at one another, wondering what our friends would say. Jokes and jeers were certainly cast at us. We who had desired to gain spiritual knowledge in a quick and easy manner had been whipped for our pains; we had taken on the character of our teacher and had degenerated; we had been dogmatic and had neglected the important aspects of material life; considering ourselves the elect, for that was the term S. had used, we had imagined the texture of our souls finer and our clay more holy than the common clay of mortals—but when we gazed more deeply into the mirrors of our minds we were shocked to find how swiftly we had descended; the reflection certainly did not flatter us. Nevertheless we felt that we had gained an invaluable experience, and that we at least had escaped before it was too late; not remaining in the society of S. as so many others did, who, with a knowledge of his character, still clung to him and obeyed him in all things. Also we still had a friend in M., who had been quietly waiting, listening patiently to our little dogmatisms, watching our childish and superior air of wisdom, and keeping silent.

So a week later I wrote to M., telling him all, for I felt that after the fall of the curtain over our small spiritual tragedy I had lost all things; love had gone, faith had gone, hope had gone. My mental pilgrimage had led me to a precipice over which I had nearly fallen. The star I had followed had not burgeoned into a great flame, but had dwindled into a mote of light barely perceptible, and it was only through the aid of M. that I believed I could awaken a new courage and enthusiasm. And in response to my letter, M. asked me to visit him; and when doing so I asked him in the same manner as so many other pupils had asked their teachers throughout the ages, for knowledge and understanding of spiritual things.

That evening he gave me the first lesson in the Divine Science, and from that period has helped me to understand a fragment of his vast knowledge. Though great as it is, he says it is but little and that he is of a Brotherhood whose knowledge is immense, and who are the true governing council of this sphere.

THE ARMY OF DREAMS

With banners of flame the singing hosts go marching forth from the shadowy cities, from night-enveloped forests and from the villages of the valleys. Yet soundlessly they tread, for they are the noble dreams of the slumberers, chanting the hymn of the spirit. Pinions of gold enrobe them, shot with slender veins of sparkling colour, while above each brow glows a slim lily of fire, and cresting each flagstaff is a dove. From the eternal mountains a song has flowed forth, beating its rhythmic tones against the sealed gates of humanity's heart. For ages had it throbbed and charged its mighty chords against these unopened doors, and now the gates are shattered, bringing release to the immortal dreams.

Part Two

PREFACE

Here, in the second part of this work, I shall relate the various experiences, many of which I know will sound impossible and fantastic to the highest degree, through which I passed while under the tuition of my teacher; though much is not said, for there are many secrets that may not be written down, and if written, would sound much more fantastic than even the strange incidents I shall endeavour to describe.

The fantastic improbabilities of today become the obvious and commonplaces of tomorrow. Today, many investigators are striving to solve some of the strange secrets and powers jealously guarded by the mind. What does the mind hold? What does the mind hide? The crude answers of yesterday will not suffice; the retort and the test-tube are not sufficiently delicate nor subtle enough to solve these mysteries.

The investigators in the science of hypnotism have evoked strange states of consciousness that prove conclusively the existence of powers that contradict the mechanistic theories of the Universe.

The Psychical Research Society has had for many years demonstrations of a supernormal nature.

And with the knowledge that we are all seeking a certain illumination regarding the mysteries of the mind, M. has suggested to me that he desired to contribute another aspect in relation to the mind; an occult aspect that, so far as he knows, has not been given to the world before. He has suggested that I relate those mental experiences through which he took me in my search for occult knowledge. And it is with that end in view that I describe some of those adventures when journeying into the realms of the mind.

WHEN EARTH AWAKENS

Because Earth has journeyed through the long, dark roads of Time, and in her pilgrimage has been plundered by the highwaymen of greed, who have robbed her of her beauty and robed her in the ragged garments of their devising, they should not think that Earth has forgotten, or that her protectors, God and the gods, are asleep. The eyes of Earth have watched, and the soul of Earth has waited. Filled with an inward power terrible in its strength, she has sometimes fed her anger on the debaucheries of men, destroying them utterly in a few moments. But in this age when love and faith are ashes, when the eidolon of Cleverness is seated in the chair of Wisdom, belief in God and in the soul of Earth are looked upon as the illusions of the ignorant. The slim whorls of music fluttering from the pipes of Pan have only been heard by the moon-englamoured poet and by the love-sick maid. And because man has lost this inheritance of intuition and the gift of imagination, he lives according to the laws of his passions and desires, hiding beneath the pall of negation those more sensitive and finer powers that once reigned supreme within him. Now he listens to the orations of his brigand passions, who strive to have him wreck that which they hate, and that beauty which would harm them most.

But the dark lanes upon which Earth has moved so long have an end, and beyond await the patient gods, each with a gift for the tired pilgrim. Their accolades shall bring to her again that pristine rapture. One shall sing to the choir of the elements a new symphony; one with a ewer of gold shall lave her in a new sweetness;

another shall wake within her the sleeping powers of magic and wisdom; and another shall lead her to their ancient temples wherein man again may become their priest and servant.

CHAPTER ONE
VISIONS AND MAGIC

Before I relate my occult experiences, I think a chapter dealing with the various visions I have seen will be of interest in relation to those things seen later on with the aid of M.

Whether the visions of the imagination are as substantial upon their own planes of manifestation as the things seen by the physical eye, within this world, I leave to the judgment of the reader. Further on I endeavour to explain the reason why I believe they are as real as the elements of our own planet, in the light of that new knowledge taught to me by M.

As I saw them, they had as great a reality and a much greater beauty than anything this Earth has ever had, within the knowledge of present-day humanity. These grandeurs were not seen in sleep, but were sometimes seen by the aid of an intense concentration, though more often unexpectedly, and with a deliberate desire to know what beauty lay hidden beyond the narrow range of the physical eye. These wonders dawned within my mind, clear-cut and spontaneously, and possessed an atmosphere that lifted me up and filled me with an almost unbearable ecstasy. I know other students have seen these hidden and holy places, and they have related in their own works the forms these glimmering and coruscating gems of the gods took (see A.E., *Candle of Vision*).

But they who have seen such wonders, though admired for their powers of imagination by those people who have never attempted to awaken this gift of clearer sight that dwells within all, have been frequently looked upon as unbalanced in mind; just as the person born blind cannot conceive the existence of colour, so these mentally blind people, being in the majority, question the sanity of those few people who have developed the gift of finer sight.

Often, through the aid of clairvoyance, friends have given me detailed descriptions of places they had never visited, and which I alone knew. Possibly that manner of seeing is telepathy, a form of wireless picture which I think has been more or less proved. Then, is it not possible that the places I am about to describe have also a real existence? The difference being that they are made of a rarer substance and belong to a different order of vibration. Here I am not speaking of the mental plane, for I do not know upon what plane these beings and temples gleam; though it is quite probable that many of these places are on the mental realms. For they possessed that purity and magnificence that only a higher realm could contain.

In these visions it should be remembered M. was not by my side, for some of these were seen before I had met him. Furthermore, seeing these places and going to them are two different things. M. took me to certain places mentioned in the chapter dealing with the mind. What I saw, I saw alone, sometimes when walking the London streets, sometimes seated on bus-tops, sometimes when walking in the country. And there was one unforgettable day when I saw for many hours a land entitled "The Joyous Land"; but that was many years ago, and the shining panorama is dimmed by the mist of the years, though the glow of that day still lingers on, though becoming ever fainter.

The most beautiful vision I have ever yet seen was a

temple of fire. It was a building that seemed endowed with life, formed from an intangible substance that throbbed and trembled like the plucked strings of a harp; and the force that gave it being seemed to live within the majestic columns that flared upwards. The windows were rimmed with a mass of glowing, fiery flowers, whose cores and petals of gold drooped downwards, clustered around with slim tendrils of finely spun flame. And the senses of my spirit laved in the ecstasy that streamed from every part of its glory, while music and perfume seemed blended into one, and I also felt as though I had melted into its warm and sweet life. A serenity never felt since enfolded me and held me poised within its paradisial loveliness.

Only regal and god-like minds could have moulded this splendour; for it seemed as an immortal and burning hymn of worship created by them as a shrine to God. It was the crystallisation of unscorching flame, shaped into a wealth of design and imagery that intoxicated the dreamer and crowned him, temporarily, with a royalty of unsurpassable magnificence. Could the imagination of pygmy man have invented such a richness, such a detailed structure that I saw? It was not a picture painted upon canvas, but it was of three dimensions; and it was only because the strain of concentration was too great that I failed to impress upon my memory many of its details. Otherwise I might have written a complete work solely about the innumerable designs that completed this temple.

And this vision rose like a titanic sun, blazing into the shadowy world of my mind. It was not like the breeze of a mood that lightly ripples the waters of thought and is gone. For it brought to me a realisation, a joy and coloured sweetness that flung me upward to the topmost pinnacle of aspiration; for it seemed to melt its golden beauty into my being, and, for a time, purify me.

The same night that I saw this splendour I contacted many other temples, but my clearest recollection was of a hall I named: "The Hall of Peacocks." Here the artist had used for his theme a study of three peacocks, whose tails were arched overhead like a dome, the end feathers meeting in the centre, and making a roof of golden eyes that shone and illuminated the hall. The birds were seated upon three pillars that were carved to resemble the ragged trunks of trees; while from the beak of each bird was suspended a lamp. This hall was clearly seen; and when I asked M. about it, he told me that the symbolic meaning of the peacock by the Indians was wisdom.

Another time, while seated in a friend's house, there came, almost as rapidly as lightning, a picture of a temple, dome-shaped, and with two great wings outstretched. It is an interesting incident, for about two years later, in my mental flights with M., I came to a place that was likewise winged.

Another instance of the quickness of vision occurred one afternoon while walking. I had often wondered about the annihilation of space by thought, as many times I had been shown, by the aid of clairvoyance, that thought could span immense distances much more rapidly than a ray of light. And with this idea in mind, I thought it would be an interesting experiment to concentrate upon a distant planet. Naturally I looked upon such an attempt as purely fantastic; but knowing that time and space were but mental concepts, I therefore made the experiment. I concentrated upon the planet

Mercury, and almost as quickly as I concentrated the vision of a strange building flashed before me, clear-cut and similar in outline to a Chinese pagoda, but the lines were of silver and appeared to cross one another like swords planted slantwise. This picture of the building was not the first, of course. Whether it was in Mercury could not be proved, though it is interesting to note that the architecture was, as far as I knew, original. And if the imagination could produce for me in a second's notice a complete picture and new form of architecture, then I think it must be admitted that the imagination surpasses in wonder even the miracle of traversing space to another world.

Another interesting instance of Mercury was when I attempted to write about an imaginary voyage to that globe. While I was writing my mind became almost dazed with a luminous silvery light that flowed before my inward eye. I seemed to see the elements of earth, air and water blending and weaving their essences into form, as though one saw the making of a world by a multitude of living elements. It is extremely difficult to describe a process that would need terms, and probably new senses, to be understood.

These experiences I have had and relate as I saw; though whether they are explainable through the normal processes of thought, I cannot tell. It is sufficient to me that I have had positive proof as to the truth of telepathy and other, as yet unknown, aspects of the mind, and I think psychologists would find this mental phenomena extremely difficult to solve.

I also believe telepathy in dreams to be another feature of psychology that has been greatly neglected; an aspect that might explain the meaning of some dreams without the aid of psychoanalysis. I would venture to suggest that modern science has touched only the shallow waters of the immense ocean of mind, and that the yogis and other students of the occult could relate, if they so desired, experiences, and possibly give demonstrations of things, that would leave the modern psychologist amazed and humbled.

My most interesting experience of dream-telepathy was when I dreamt that some friends of mine were greatly troubled over a letter received. I woke up somewhat anxious and then, after a little thought, dismissed the matter as only a dream. A week or two later I visited them and was told about a letter that they had received, which had given them a great deal of anxiety. The rest of the story being somewhat too remarkable to be believed, I shall not relate it. But I know it gave me an insight into the evil forces that dwell on the other planes, and in what manner they attack the forces of good, using as their instruments weak and negative people to unconsciously hurt their friends.

To return to my visions, I remember seeing one evening a most gracefully designed palace. A few moments previously I had seen the face of a being that was masculine in features, yet feminine in form, that appeared to swim in the air. And as I gazed on it, I found myself in a palace built from a strangely smooth and white material. A slender and lofty dome rose upwards, Gothic in design, but much narrower, while the doors were rounded like twin petals glowing with a wealth of pictures, and the windows were likewise. I also noticed that the columns supporting the palace were voluted, and spread smaller pillars like the branches of a tree. A night later I saw M. and told him of this place, and he said that he had also seen it. So probably in this case it was telepathy. Incidentally, I think it would be interesting to mention that of the many things I had seen in vision or dreamt, in which the details were not very clear, when telling M. he generally reminded me of some minor features that I had forgotten.

Only a few times have I met people in meditation, and they were as real to me as any of the beings that dwell upon Earth. And one never-to-be-forgotten night, while walking home, some power leaped into me and swept me up into a storm of beauty and strength. It was some great being and I can still remember its face, which was bright with a dazzling fairness, the skin like that of a lovely woman, yet filled with a power that was purely masculine. The profile held the mingled beauty of an ancient Greek and warrior Norseman. He was about eighteen feet high, and his hair was like coiling locks of fire that streamed in some unfelt wind. I have never seen him since, but the memory of his majesty can never be forgotten.

I have also heard music, but they were chords that glorified my dreams; an experience, I believe, most people have had. But one morning I woke with the last strains of some mighty song rolling away, one chord repeating itself continuously; and to me it sounded like the song of the sun as it whirled its fiery way, and I imagined such strains beating its royal rhythms into the troubled soul of humanity, and rising octave after octave, louder and louder, yet sweeter and sweeter. And as its music flowed through life, it transmuted the passions of all the living things that moved about this globe into something pure and selfless, like an ocean of music that swept all the debris and little spites into eternal oblivion, leaving a white world. And this chord lifted me up until I was bathing in a rhapsody of sound.

How can they who have experienced these things disbelieve in a greater power who is far above man? Who rules and guides him, giving his soul a little freewill, his ears a faint echo of its melodies, and his eyes the shadowy glimmer of its domains of pristine loveliness.

I think a few pages upon those powers locked up within man, and the desires of man for those things that could give him vision, would be of interest in this chapter.

One power has fascinated man even before the desire for truth, even before Time scattered his snowflakes, called the hours—and that power is magic. The magic in mythology, in the weird enchantments of Eastern tales, even in the modern fantasy of today, has always evoked a thrill and a wish in the young heart for magic rings; for the power to command genii; for the cap and cloak of invisibility; for seven-league boots, so that one could fly to the rescue of the damsel captured by the ogre; for winged steeds and magic carpets; for the hidden beauty and terror of glamorous woods; for the adventure in the hidden palace, deep in the witch-haunted forests. All these desires for romance sing in the souls of the child-hearted ones.

For there is a gallant youth, dwelling in the heart of humanity, who is spotless in heart and clad in golden and silver armour. Who, upon richly caparisoned steed, journeys through dangerous lands, slaying ogre and dragon with his magic sword. Often he is a poor lad who seeks his fortune and rescues the beautiful princess from the giant's castle with the aid of invisible cap and cunning.

And it is noticeable that within all these magical tales the plot consists of a battle between good and evil; the fairy triumphs over the witch and the knight over the wizard. No tale in which black magic has conquered white has survived the centuries; and herein lies the proof of the inherent good that dwells within man, despite his vices and weaknesses. Also the belief in that cosmic magician who watches our sufferings and comes to the rescue of the victims who are caught in the whirlpool of evil and pain, at the psychological moment, has given man the strength to fight against apparently hopeless odds. For many even today believe in magic, the magic of prayer, and the belief that the Supreme Magician will answer their despairing cries. And if we carefully study the gifts and help that comes suddenly to people sinking for the last time beneath the waters of defeat, we would be amazed to discover how numerous are these rescues. For I have investigated this subject very carefully and have found it to be almost a law, and though it is unexplainable from any scientific standpoint, yet I would say that this is a form of magic that occurs possibly daily.

I would define magic not as the working of supernatural law, but the actions of natural laws of other planes affecting our world; and romance is the result of the individual caught in the coloured webs of these laws that entwine their beauty and wonder around many today, or I should say, perhaps around all. For we live in a world of effects and in that way can truly state that all is magic; for we do not know the spirit and power that protects, aids, and even at times speaks to us from its invisible realms. But we are too engrossed in the misty follies of today that melt when found to observe these glistening threads of enchantment that wind themselves round our souls and actions. These hues and laws of another world are accepted as a matter of course and are passed by unnoticed, though when the individual reads a fairy-tale he wishes in his heart that such happenings and rescues and enchantments were true.

There are magicians who move among us today, who know of the world of causes and move in those realms with as much familiarity as they do when walking within the streets and countries of this planet; people who are unknown, yet in the possession of powers that make them the hidden governors of this world; men and women who possibly lead quiet and humble lives, yet who meet their brethren in conscious union upon another plane, and there assist to carry out the plan and purpose of their work in incarnation, and oppose the darker forces that attempt to englamour man and prevent him from carrying out his own particular work in life.

Still, we could be answered that the magic of the fairy-tale does not exist. Where is the magic carpet, the cap of invisibility, the genii and the fairies, the giants and the gods, the fair isles of enchantment? And in the following words I shall endeavour to illustrate in what manner these things exist.

Man is like a captain who has closed his eyes. They are not bandaged, but he will not make the effort to open them. And slowly he drifts, his body like a ship whose sails are blown by a myriad perverse moods that flow from strange and unknown regions. Some reigned over by destructive and forbidding monarchs, who delight in sending tempests to drive the vessels upon submerged rocks and against granite-armoured cliffs; and others reigned over by gentle and humble princes of

God, who seek to drive the vessels to the placid bays and havens of the immense continents of Truth and Beauty. And according to the desires of the captain so follows the breeze or the hurricane. It is only when the captain nears the rock or the port that he suddenly opens his eyes, and then he sees towards what manner of land he had been voyaging. He also discovers that he had carried a full cargo of undreamt-of treasure, among which were gifts that could have helped him to have made a swifter and much more interesting journey.

There were instruments of magic that had lain in various parts of the vessel ever since the voyage had begun, but they were unnoticed because they appeared commonplace and old-fashioned. Here was a flask tightly sealed, upon which was inscribed a symbol. Were he to have opened it he would have disenchanted a genii as powerful and as wonderful as the spirit that haunts the Arabian fairy-tale; a power that could have lifted the ship above the boundaries of Earth; a power that could have opposed all the unknown laws of Earth; a power transcending much that man nowadays considers irresistible. For the genii of the Orient is no fantasy, and his power is based upon a force that sleeps within the soul of man; a magical force known throughout the ages to all mystics and occultists. All humanity possess this force, though it is fortunate for the majority that it has not been awakened, for it can make man a devil or a god, according as it is used, whether for good or for evil. So in a way it is well that the captain does not open this flask, though if he had made the effort he might have succeeded in unlocking this power.

The next instrument of magic is a telescope, old and long ago discarded and folded in a leather case, and because of its age it is looked upon by science as a relic and curiosity and of little use. But were the captain to open it he would find it full of magic, a magic that could annihilate space and time. With it he could see what was taking place thousands of miles away, and thousands of years ago. He could see what was to come, for by the aid of such a power he could awaken the gift of prophecy and foretell the disasters and joys to come. Again, he could see the Fall of Babylon and the pomp of gleaming cities not yet erected upon Earth, though planned in the world of the spirit. For the telescope of clairvoyance, an instrument that many men of today scoff at, when fully opened possesses powers as splendid as the most perfect scientific instrument of modern times.

And the cloak of invisibility, is that possible? Of that particular power I am writing in the chapter devoted to my mental travels, and with that one can link the seven-league boots and the magic carpet, for all the magic methods of travel written about in fairy-tales are but the symbols of certain powers hidden within man.

And the haunted woods and forests? Let man open his eyes and he will see wonders and fantasy that would be beyond the storyteller's power to tell; while man is the prince or the poor youth who ever seeks to rescue that princess, the spirit, enchanted in the castle of the clay. And the enchanted isles? When the imagination is fed with the golden dews of the spirit, then our awakened eyes shall see the glamour that surrounds each island of our small globe.

I believe all our inventions and discoveries are but poor imitations of the hidden forces sleeping in the most humble of savages and the most regal of thinkers, and that all our instruments of science but the crutches man is compelled to use till he can awaken those inner kingly and godlike powers.

THE WARRIORS OF ETERNITY

The white citadel is invaded; the houses of alabaster and marble, and the monuments once haloed in an argent radiance are dimmed with shadows, as the wide, sun-bathed streets ring with the voices of battling, gold-helmed warriors. Yet no fury of black-bearded and ape-like enemy are they fighting, but monsters belched forth from the dark lips of cavern and chasm that lie beneath the foundations of the city.

With steel-hard talons, welded to rippling pillars of hair and muscle, they plunge amid the javelin and sword-lit throng, who, with firm-lipped faces, erect and clean-limbed, hurl their weapons, like silver shafts of fire, against their attackers. For aeons have they been battling, yet neither side victorious, neither side defeated. For they come from the infinite spaces of night and day, gathering in the ageless city of the mind, in whose centre stands a tower, smooth and slender, like a frozen moonbeam, wherein a godlike captain, with locks of light, and eyes deeper than twin tarns, that are like orbed doors opening upon quiet immensities, gazes meditatively upon the passionate hosts. He is the divine architect who builds and plans, even as they are fighting, for the day when a truce shall be declared between the opponents, and the dark ones return to their world beneath the city.

CHAPTER TWO

HEALTH

The teachings given to me by M. were the importance of health, exercise and moderation in all things. He also taught me the manner in which one should sit and walk, his lessons in walking particularly interesting me, as I had heard long before a strange tale regarding a yogi and his would-be pupil.

A young man of the East once earnestly desired to become an initiate in the Divine Mysteries, and for that purpose approached a yogi who was seated at the end of a long room. As the young man approached, the yogi watched him and simply told him to return within a year. The young man left and studied earnestly and deeply, and at the appointed time returned to the yogi; but ere he reached him he was told to go back to his studies and return a year later. Wonderingly, the student did so, and the year passed swiftly in his attempts to learn wisdom. Then again he came to the yogi, who told him to go home yet once more. At the conclusion of the third year, he visited the yogi; and the yogi, gazing at him, told him that now he was fit to become his disciple and explained to his new pupil the reason for his many dismissals. The yogi could tell what spiritual illumination he had received by the manner of his walk, and he knew whether he had received certain knowledge or otherwise.

And M. taught me the same thing, giving me instances wherein one could tell whether the animal or the spirit ruled the person. M. said that the pupil learned much by observation; that the simple little things disregarded by the majority are sometimes to the occult student of much greater importance than the obvious incident that attracts the crowd. To learn from everybody and from everything was impressed upon me. And here I may mention that the mystic and dreamer who moves through a continual mist loses much knowledge through his disinterest in human and natural affairs. The occultist must have a mind as well trained for observation as the scientist, with the exception that he uses a different method for experiment; his testing instruments being thought and feeling, and the other hidden senses that scientists do not believe exist.

The occultist has trained his feeling of sensitivity to an extraordinary degree, and therefore can feel the unseen motives that influence an individual or a crowd. For instance, he could possibly tell you that though a certain person had committed a murder, it did not prove that the person doing so had done it with his own free-will; quite possibly an obsessing entity had entered into the criminal. The person who suddenly commits suicide at a spot where others had done so, and this has often happened, could, quite possibly, have been obsessed by the beings who had destroyed their bodies previously and were therefore earthbound; or they may have been drawn into the current of emotion that lingered there, for I think it is well known that old influences remain long after the actors have vanished. Another aspect of crime can be caused by hypnosis at a distance. I could give many reasons for certain actions and not one of them need be the same; though, I admit, neither could any of them have been proved to the satisfaction of the court or the coroner, who use different methods of examination and give generally obvious explanations which, often to the occultist, may be incorrect.

When we speak of the occultist of course it is understood that we also include the mystic, for the true occultist has to develop the emotional principles simultaneously with the mental principles, for he must be balanced if he wishes to understand the experiences through which he passes and the truths of the world. We have met so many unbalanced students that we feel it is necessary to state this, for much time is wasted when we refuse to accept the fact that we have incarnated into a world in order to understand that world. The occultist is not an anchorite, except at certain times when he has to develop certain powers, and then it is necessary for him to dwell in a quiet part of the world and live as near to nature as possible; but many students confuse the practical side of life and the mystical. The occultist cannot dwell in a hermitage all his life; neither, if he wishes to develop his inner powers, can he live in the cities all his life. It is possible that the most practical, the most healthy and matter-of-fact person whom you imagine to be the most mundane may more likely be the keen occultist than the most dreamy, un-vital and eccentric person who calls himself a student of such a subject, for this person may be as far away from his true goal as this planet is from the sun. Eccentricity, pose and conversations dealing with delirious visions are most unsatisfactory proof that the person is an initiate; and we should say further that such a person should be avoided by those who wish to possess a healthy mind, for there are mental diseases that are also catching.

Later on in my studies M. taught me the value of a certain breathing exercise, a form of regular breathing that I have practiced continually ever since, and which has helped me greatly in giving me a clear mind and strength to study much that is taught me. It also gave me a certain rhythm and control that was necessary for me when I visited the mental planes, about which I have devoted a later chapter. But about breathing, I here quote a commentary from the book mentioned in the chapter entitled "The Meeting":

By concentration in meditation upon a given subject, and by the EFFORT of regular breathing, the inhalation and exhalation occupying the same space of time, the mind may be held so that it is not subject to other thought than that pertaining to the object or symbol of expression about which man desires knowledge. And if man will persist in this practice, he can enter into a harmonious relationship with the Divinity within and from that source can gain knowledge, which is the result of the soul's own experience while passing through the higher and lower states of matter.

At the same time, if man will concentrate upon the highest, he can evoke from within self that Solar Force and Power which, if directed upwards, will awaken and revitalise those ganglia or organs of perception hitherto withheld from his use. If it be true, "From God we came, to God we return," life is but the attainment of that consciousness which is of God. And man is therefore shut out from the knowledge of his true being and estate until he seeks at-one-ment with his own Divine Life-Principle, and its evolution and manifestation in him.

Thus concentration in meditation, holding the mind receptive to the Divinity within and in a positive attitude of repression to all outside thought, is seen to be an exalted form of prayer or communion with God, Nature, whereby man may become a sharer in the wonder of God's Omnipotence and recover his lost Sovereignty. (Villars, *Comte de Gabalis*, p. 56)

Much stated in this quotation I have endeavoured to follow, with results that I have mentioned previously. Meditation and breathing produced within me an increasing sensitivity, which had I developed without an additional strength of physical well-being, would have produced an intolerable suffering. I mentioned this increase of feeling to M., and he told me that now I could realise what one who has been a student for many years must suffer; "but," he continued, "the gods would not permit you to feel beyond your powers of resistance."

I have had proof of this increased sensitivity, for I have felt mental and emotional atmospheres as clearly as one would feel the waves when swimming. And that is the reason why I have mentioned previously that the occultist uses different instruments of perception, and therefore knows the inner powers and motives that have guided persons to commit crimes and do strange things.

Also I think it can now be understood why I say the mystic, who has not developed balance but has developed an ever-increasing sensitivity, is liable through his being too negative to become, like many Spiritualists, obsessed.

In speaking about the results attained regarding these various occult exercises, I have never yet met a genuine student who did not possess a singular and powerful vitality upon all planes, M. particularly possessing in a marked degree all these aspects.

In relation to breathing M. once said to me:

The energy derived from breathing harmonises one's conditions and gives one that singular energy which is beyond the ordinary conceptions of the human mind. For, by breathing, we stimulate certain active principles within our being and derive energy from their higher mental counterpart. The act of occult breathing is like a man throwing a rope to a centre of still finer energy, and that energy pulling you over to harmonise you with the nature of its essences.

M. always impressed upon me the relativity which exists between one's higher and lower counterpart.

One [he said] always has a crutch to walk with, but one seldom knows how to use it. For man's best friend is his own sovereign ruler, for it kindles that fire which illumines man's intelligence. But it is easy to speak of these things, only what a struggle it is to acquire the use of one's own higher possessions.

I think in these few principles the student will find much that will be of use to him in his attempt to solve some of the problems that beset him, when first adventuring through the fields of illusion and towards that great Reality that ever watches the pioneering souls.

THE ISLE OF TIME

Forever the great outgoing waves of eternity charge the rattling and tumbling pebbles strewn on the beach of Time; gathering the weeds of incident, the wreckage of the hours; washing away the villages and cities of the years, endlessly, relentlessly, into the vast ocean of the spirit. While upon other incoming tides, the chariot waves, whose guides and masters are the gods, bring barques heavy with cargoes back from voyaging to the white realms of the spirit. Old are these ships, yet luminous with the shadows of forsaken powers; and into these ports and bays of Time's great dominions they sail, where the myriad slaves of the years await to gather from these vessels strange cargoes.

Many of these slaves are deaf and blind, and many are shackled, but they obey their masters, who are their Higher Selves, and build according to a preordained plan. Clumsily they construct, from the materials the waters brought them, villages with narrow, ill-lit lanes, grey houses and grey castles; creating cities, but dulling their beauty with that garish display that only the crude mind could conceive. But other slaves whose shackles hang more lightly upon their limbs, and who are less deaf to the diapason of Eternity's waters, understand who it is that commands them to build; understand that the cargoes these ships have brought are the old deeds wrought in past lives. And with knowledge they build once again, upon the site that older tides had swept, lovely cities that reflect in the eternal ocean new imagery, new wonders and glories; and though they know that these splendours they have erected will also be washed away, yet they also know that the illumination of these golden structures will leave an eternal gleam and greater wisdom within their deathless spirits.

CHAPTER THREE
VARIOUS OCCULT TEACHINGS

In this chapter I shall write down a few of those I teachings M. gave me at various periods, with the addition of a few commentaries of my own. What M. has said I put in quotation marks.* As I know that the occult student is always interested in fresh knowledge in regard to this study, I write these in the hope that he will find some solution to certain problems. I know that in many cases I have not given a complete answer, but it would be impossible to do so as it would mean a departure from the true character of this book, which deals primarily with certain teachings in regard to the mental plane. Therefore, though this chapter may appear to be somewhat disconnected, I hope, nevertheless, it will still attract the student.

I think the teachings in regard to initiation obviously come first, and I here quote the answer M. gave me regarding that question.

> Within the soul of each mortal dwells a watcher, one who waits patiently for the time when his charge will cry out for a consciousness of the divine realities, and when that occurs, the inner watcher guides the seeker into a series of experiences that will perfect and make him fit to enter the temples of Truth. Wherever the seeker dwells, whether he be white, yellow or black, whether he dwells in a hovel or a palace, directly he desires to become a helper for humanity and work in unity with the laws of the spirit, directly he listens

* [In this edition, the sayings of M. are set as block quotations.]

to the compelling voice of intuition that bids him seek beyond the glamour of events, and he obeys it; then the watcher within takes him upon a voyage that can only end when the seeker has found his own. But when guiding him, the watcher also gives to him various keys, keys that will open each of the seven doors that lead into ancient chambers, wherein can be found books written by the other selves of the past, works wherein are inscribed the symbols of divine powers. Only by perseverance and relentless pursuit can the seeker attain his desires. For in his aspiration for initiation, he must not permit his energies to be frittered away in the mental clamour and voices of parasitic and vague interests that are shaped from mist and bring only temporary nourishment. For initiation consists of discovering one's own limitations, though one also discovers an affinity to the elements of nature and the universe. And a time comes in his occult studies when he enters through the curtains of air, and he discovers new regions, new laws and truths, which he endeavours to build into his character; and possess powers that can demonstrate to humanity the existence of higher kingdoms and forces.

Truth need not come to a man after he is dead, for Heavenly powers can be sought for and found while he yet walks the Earth. As I have mentioned elsewhere, each civilisation has not perished in vain, for their powers, though sleeping, still possess vitality. Man incarnates in order to gain new experiences and also an extension of consciousness that like eternally burning lamps will bring to him an inner and perpetual illumination. Furthermore, when seven different sources give to the seeker's mental atmosphere their filaments, he then possesses those powers that will give to him a rounded consciousness.

I mention later on in this chapter certain knowledge regarding symbols which I think the reader can relate to these principles of initiation.

One peculiarity about human nature has often puzzled man—why good deeds and thoughts should so often be returned by evil. Why people who have given love and affection should have those gifts returned by hate. Often people meet others to whom they are attracted, and, after becoming friends, find that their love has evoked an evil quality in that friend, which causes them untold sufferings. "Why," they ask, "should a friend I love rend me?"

I once asked M. if he could give me a reason for this strange aspect of life, and was answered to this effect:

There are two types of humanity upon this planet, commonly known as the white and the black, or the brothers of the right hand and the brothers of the left hand. You will find the answer I am giving you in most of the sacred books written by the great religious teachers of the past, but I will give you the reason in my own words.

There was one type that responded to the call of the Reality, was breathed upon and sent into matter. It is named the "white soul," for it responded to the call. The other monad did not do so, but followed the natural phases of evolution, and is known by the occultist as the black or the oppressor; but it is needed for the evolution of the white, for it plunges humanity through great ranges of experience, until in man's mind is generated a desire to seek the real source of its being.

These oppressors, in the course of time, will also obey the call, and receive the breath of immortality: meaning, I think, that while they are black they lack that spiritual consciousness possessed by the white.

It takes an occult student many years before he can determine, at a glance, the symbol on their brows. And the student's relationship to these people is not governed by the heart, but by wisdom. As the teacher of Galilee said, "Side with thine adversary" (Matthew 5:25); also that one should have "the wisdom of a serpent" (Matthew 10:16).

It is in the nature of these oppressors to hate, for you evoke a power latent in them, which they use in order to uncover your own weaknesses, and which they exploit when having done so. By giving them love, you also give them a power which they may use in order to injure you; they recognise the weaknesses within you, and act in many ways that is good for one. Often they have unfrocked the priest. It is wise [M. concluded] not to antagonise them.

Before I wrote the chapter dealing with my mental journeys, M. gave me a number of notes relating to the mind; and I think it will be of greater interest to place them in this chapter dealing with occult teachings.

The sun awakens the mind to diverse activities, whereas the moon stills it and gives it power to absorb the materials of the inner self's more divine Wisdom.

The moon has its part in the mental activities, for

it teaches the lower mind the sound which can unite it to its higher mind and bring it mental balance; for the power of the mind is derived from its attachment to its solar and lunar orbits, for in the light of the sun it develops its fight of mental activities; but the moon plays its part in producing depths of expression.

When we derive nourishment from Nature, we develop a power similar to the power of a white magician, for Nature is the self-developed mental body of the innermost; but that spiritual power which Nature guards is not given to one unless one has passed into the inner states of being. (In the chapter upon mental travels, I describe such a voyage.) This is why we go upon mental journeys and leave the body, in order to contact this mind stuff which is of a finer nature than the so-called mind stuff of man, though it is subject to the lower mental atmosphere of himself and others; all the thoughts and questions and worries of humanity that like a cloud arise between the true mind of each man and the false. The pupil must analyse his own self and seek the material of his own mind in order to pass into the material atmosphere of Nature's substantial embodiment.

When I travelled out of the body M. continually told me to aspire in order that I reach a certain atmosphere, which was a truer expression of my inner and higher being.

Man has within him the elements of fire, air, water and earth; and the power to attain to the mental consciousness of each of these different elemental spheres, for within him are the corresponding seats of government by which these elements can be controlled.

In the chapter entitled "The Meeting," I speak of a spiritual aristocracy who have learned to use such powers.

There are many people who retain a knowledge of such elemental consciousness and can see things from the elemental plane as well as from the human plane; a gift particularly found with inventors, who have a faint perception of Nature's truths, and who thus seek to harness these unknown laws of Nature. Often, many people intuitively stumble upon Nature's secrets but lack the scientific training to materialise this knowledge. This ignorance must be surmounted before man can become a magician. Therefore, even our experimental science has its uses, and even the materialistic scientist, in his efforts to discover Nature's secrets, also creates a path to God.

Only listen to the inner Self for instruction, for many of the recognised laws of science are falsely explained. It is interesting to note that many of the explanations that the ancients possessed for certain phenomena, though laughed at and scorned by modern scientists, are yet slowly and unwillingly being accepted. An interesting instance in regard to the power of the moon may be mentioned. As is well known, the ancients and people of the mediaeval periods stated that if certain things were gathered at a certain time when the moon was at a certain phase, the gathered herbs or any other particular thing done beneath its beams would possess or lack a certain influence. These beliefs sounded so improbable that scientists did not even trouble to investigate. And now I read that the moon, besides possessing an influence upon the tides, does produce a difference in trees cut down at certain of its phases. And if these influences work upon trees, why not upon herbs? How the ancients knew these things, I cannot tell. Quite probably they used these finer senses that I have spoken about so often. As scientific investigation proceeds, I think many more so-called superstitions will compel the world of science to change its views regarding the poetical superstitions of the ancients. When I read the arrogant manner with which certain scientists dismiss, through sheer intolerance, things discovered by those who have not earned University degrees, I am amazed. For, above all, I believe that all search for knowledge should be impersonal. And the manner with which scientists oppose new and ancient theories is sufficient proof that they are not so much in love with truth as they are with themselves.

M.'s method of teaching was completely inductive. Also he would try to take me to those realms where the mind found its power for a higher and more defined expression. The principal topic was seldom of a personal character; dealing more or less with the nearer and clearer fields of thought. He would tell me that when we find the mind unhampered of its discordant objective nature, we can then bring into use a finer mental atmosphere; a stimulating and more powerful force of thought that gives one the power of vision when out of the body. Roughly speaking, he divided the mind substance into three different atmospheres through which I had to pass; they were like mental sheaths. He told me to watch the character of thoughts which entered into my mind, analyse them, and realise that these thoughts had a higher counterpart of expression; which was of the nature of an emotion, for the student must learn to translate the "thought-emotions," which are sent to one while on the inner and higher planes, so that the student can in time translate "thought-emotion" into thought as recognised by the lower mind; for the language of these higher planes is by the "thought-emotions," and it takes a student many years to be able to understand such a language. And the same process which M. had passed through in learning, he strove to teach me.

Many artists, he told me, intuitively translate these emotions of the higher planes. I have noticed myself that, when I am inspired, it is not a question of thought so much as a form of ecstasy, which I think is the language of the spirit and the higher mind. It will be noticed that, before each chapter, I have placed a prologue, which in style and expression is totally different from my normal writing. The critic would say that I had attempted to be a stylist and artificial; and that supposition would be totally incorrect, for I but expressed the higher emotions into, I hope, fitting though stumbling language. For I had learnt through M's teachings and from various experiments that I could contact many different states of consciousness, and that these states would alter my method of expression; and on experimenting I found that I could do so.

As mentioned previously, I had little knowledge as to my abilities in literature. My tentative efforts had been expended in prose of a fantastic and imaginative nature; also in arguments, ponderous and philosophic. But after meeting M., my aspirations changed; and I was amazed to find how great a joy dwelt in the writing of verse, which also needed so many qualities; such as logic, concentration, patience, persistence and clear-headedness. And I once asked M. if he could give me what he considered a good definition of fine art, and here I quote his reply:

The words of a great teacher are direct and concise, and seemingly spoken without effort. A poem from the higher spheres of being is determined energy simplified. It causes one's mind to awaken into the nature of the sphere from which the poem was derived, and thus causes the mind to harmonise itself with the higher counterpart of this poem. And for that reason a great poem does a great work, for it helps the mind to break through the lower mental environment and brings it to the sphere where self-thought can be engendered.

It is most important for an artist not to show his work until it is completed, for many unseen spirits, dwelling on the lower planes, can then see the work when the artist speaks about it and shows it to his friends. Also it is like bringing into incarnation an unfinished body; and the many ignorant forces that surround man upon the lower planes are only too willing to prevent the artist from completing his work, or else contacting him to a lower source of art so that if he does complete it, it will not be as fine and as finished as the artist had in his original inspiration conceived it to be. I think it is very noticeable that many people who speak a great deal about what they intend doing, seldom complete their task.

Again M. says:

In the higher planes, the artist has built up his own material, and many times assistance is given him in order that he may contact his own creative energy which he has established on the inner planes. Many poems are but poor translations of the poet's real inner themes, and often when out of the body one finds a poet studying his own poems and endeavouring to bring them down into a more material form so that he may remember them when in the Earth-awakened consciousness.

I have mentioned elsewhere that I have often read complete poems in my dream life, and even now I have a recollection of their verse forms and subjects.

Sometimes the poet reads his own works on the higher planes, then descends with it to a middle plane and strives to make this poem correspond with the intelligence of this middle plane; and here as well as on the higher plane he receives the aid of a teacher who attempts to impress the artist's mind with his material when he awakens on the physical plane. It is always the aim of these teachers who assist the artist to bring into incarnation a work of the nature of the higher spheres. Also they endeavour to help the artist to keep that same vitality of thought-emotions that the work possesses on the higher realms.

There exists a fraternity of wise men, a group who have governed this planet ever since it came into being, who are detailed to watch, protect and teach those students who are deemed strong enough to become instruments for the cup of the spirit: instruments through which the consciousness of the reality may manifest; and these students are the torch-bearers who will stimulate the minds of humanity

to self-thought. The range of these helpers is unlimited; through the arts, through science, through
commerce, anyone who earnestly seeks can become
an instrument of greater or lesser degree. Even the
cheap Christmas-card is as important for the less
cultured mind as the masterpiece is for the cultured.
Ella Wheeler Wilcox has been a great stimulant to
thousands of mill girls who needed encouragement.
For there are ministering souls for all. The cup of
the spirit is never withheld from those who seek to
give their best to humanity. Once a great American
teacher travelled from China to minister to the prayer
of a half-breed Indian, dwelling somewhere in the
wilds of Labrador, and who was calling for spiritual
help. This teacher with his pupil took a long sledge-
journey to give the first instruction to this soul crying
out in the wilderness.

To return to the artist who has intuitively used the
occult method of art expression. M. mentioned James
McNeill Whistler as an instance of one who had developed that finer perception, the higher mentality. For
he shadowed forth a new perception, which, though
in the beginning was not understood and was derided,
was later on ultimately accepted by the majority of
artists. He was, as M. said, a forerunner who came to
teach the world to see.

The material essence of mind with which I became
familiar when travelling out of the body is the mirror
in which the higher emotions and thoughts of people
are read. But it is often beclouded. For the reason why
people cannot see and receive impressions and thoughts
of other people is because this finer atmosphere is

enshrouded by its lower counterpart, in which dwells the larvae of intolerance and the debris of unthinking minds.

M. also emphasised the necessity for care when speaking upon matters dealing with the well-being of others, for he sought to understand the motives rather than the actions of his pupils; an aspect I have mentioned elsewhere, and which in the light of this new knowledge can now be understood, for the emotions expressed by the higher portions of the mind are sometimes disturbed and deflected by the debris of other and lower minds. Proving, I think, that few persons truly express themselves, for they cannot reach that true part of themselves that would give them a new outlook and understanding of their inner beings. Concentration is the key to motive-action, and one should hold true to the inner and higher emotions, regardless of what the critics might say. Also, one should obey the commanding voice of intuition, for the intuition never betrays you as the heart too often does.

And in answer to further questions regarding the mind and how to attain to such a clear and true state of consciousness, M. said:

You should tell the world that there is a great spiritual consciousness that has never departed from its members. In the past there had been a great civilisation, and though its members had been scattered and assembled, and scattered again and again, yet every member calls to its own; this father and mother who have so carefully nourished them. And today there is still an underlying chord stretching from its golden age to those subjects deemed worthy of its notice, for this civilisation has carried itself in its evolution into our present and even into our future, and if we still desire to attain to its consciousness, and the knowledge of the plan and purpose of its manifestation; and if we have eyes to see, we can perceive that in our minds there is still a filament connecting us with the object of this great consciousness, which is the creation of ideals, *nourished by Nature*, and fostered by the stern, restless spirit of eternity.

It has today its place and manifestation in our mental world, and it has given to those who will walk the Path leading to Right Activity a knowledge which will liberate them from being the slave to that mental debris with which they have encumbered themselves. For its great ideal may become the teacher of all mankind. For the ideal that has been given to this great and incarnated consciousness was to establish in men's minds a knowledge of just relationship between man and man. The ignorant may say, "But what can this aristocracy of mind have to do with just judgment and the ruling of the world?" And the answer is: Eventually a great ideal will rule the world and no heart will be safe from it.

Just as man's body is nourished by Nature's elements or products, similarly will his mind be nourished if he will but draw upon those finer elements of mind which illuminate man's mental body. If by aspiration and desire man seeks to resume his sovereignty in Nature, he can derive mental stimulation and power from the corresponding mentalities of which Nature is endowed. Man's mind is but a fulcrum which he can adjust to the many mental attributes of Nature.

My teacher has constantly impressed upon me the importance of studying and becoming acquainted with the mentalities, which are of fire, air, water and earth. We can divide the mind into three determinative factors to assist us in our mental development, which I have mentioned previously; also it must establish itself in its true place and position in Nature's consciousness in order to become conscious of its determined plan in evolution; and it must assume its determinative faculty or power in Nature, for its ideal is determined, and that ideal must become known to the student ere he can take his true place and assert this ideal in Nature.

If you could only realise [M. said] how just Nature is as a lawgiver, you would not break her commandments. For we go to the Great Mother for knowledge of the laws of contrasted energies, as energy is the keynote to success. A knowledge in mental and contrasted energies breaks down the will to power, that power and knowledge which magicians have sought to attain but can never get through lack of that nourishment which the Great Mother alone reveals to her true sons.

As I have mentioned in the short note upon the higher sylphs, they will not permit the mentally and morally unclean to enter their pure and higher kingdoms, for these powers look upon man as a destructive creature; and I think rightly so. Imagine these evil powers, the black magicians or the brothers of the left hand, entering these kingdoms; what a terrible power for destruction they would possess. And I think if man questions the existence of the gods and the elemental peoples, the answer to such a question: "Why have they not seen them?" lies in this paragraph. For how many are there who are fit to enter these kingdoms?

M. continues further:

The masters of courage are not blinded by selfish egotism. They have no personality, for they need none,
as they are directed and individualised as a unit, a
united consciousness which will be truly recognised
by those who have partaken of Nature's wisdom. The
masters of courage are needed, for they still stimulate minds to assume their lawful heritage: meaning
those minds who strive to work in harmony with the
laws of Nature, and who strive to unlock that source
of mental and spiritual creative energy. The mind is
an expression of an ideal which fosters and nourishes
mankind in order to unify man with Mother Earth,
give nourishment to Mother Air, and slake the thirst
of those who seek to pass the illusion planes.

Our physical bodies derive nourishment from food
supplied by Nature. Do people realise where their mental
nourishment comes from? Though I am not permitted
to state fully the planes and the method in which we
take mental nourishment, I may state that such nourishment does not come from the physical food that
we take into our bodies, but from a totally different
source.

Nowadays, the psychoanalyst states that nearly all
our ideas, our inventions, our inspirations are but the
products of transmuted sex-emotions, made beautiful
or otherwise by the actions of the subconscious mind.
Transmuted sex-force, I venture to suggest, might be
but the energy necessary to commence and complete
our artistic conceptions or inventions. It might be but
the physical power that gives strength to concentration, but not to inspiration—inspiration coming from

a totally different source. Let us conceive the mind as a wireless instrument that needs a certain amount of energy to time it up in order that it may catch the finer vibrations; that energy used may be the sex-force. Obviously the inspiration is coloured and moulded by the personality. There is another aspect of the subconscious that I think is very puzzling, and in the light of M.'s teachings may solve the problem. The question is: How can a subconscious and automatic part of ourselves produce a unified, a perfected and harmonious masterpiece that so many geniuses of the past have created when truly inspired ? Occultists have said throughout the ages that there exists within us many self-conscious units who work in harmony and obey the commands of the sovereign spirit. Surely such a belief simplifies all the tortuous and unsatisfactory theories, since they are but theories, for the psychologists have brought forward little actually proved to be scientifically true. Scientists are so unwilling to accept the remotest possibility of something greater than themselves that they will willingly entangle themselves in a network of fantastic conceptions that are at times more improbable than the possible existence of the gods. When one experiences, as so many have experienced, these premonitions, these intuitions and the many unsolved mysteries of the soul, how foolish one would be to deny the existence of these conscious powers that call out to us continually that they do exist. If we could look upon man as a hive, from whence the bees seek honey, not alone from the nearby flowers but from flowers that blossom in unseen and foreign lands, we might have a truer and completer understanding as to the inner forces of man.

And in regard to such inner powers, I think M.'s note upon symbols will not be out of place.

Periodically, three great hierarchal forces pour upon humanity, stimulating and engendering the mind with a new creative element, giving man power to apprehend and make known to his consciousness a knowledge of laws. For instance, at one period the Assyrians and Babylonians had a true and complete knowledge of astronomy and astrology; the Egyptians, a knowledge and understanding of the hidden forces of Nature; and the Greeks, a consciousness of rhythm and beauty.

I think in regard to these hierarchal powers, such forces can easily explain the reason why humanity in different periods worshipped and created gods and symbols that were the well-defined expressions of inner powers which mankind of today have not contacted. For we must pass through a number of phases, all different in aspect. And today the forces that play upon humanity possess a different form of consciousness, which, when fully expressed, will also pass away. Though, as I mention elsewhere, they will again return in order to weave into new races their ancient and yet new form of divine expression.

Only when the great golden age again returns, M. told me, will all those muted chords of consciousness awaken and, blending harmoniously, surge into the beings of all men, making the clay a fount for the ecstasy, the fire, the wisdom and the glory of the gods.

Therefore I think it is unwise to consider the ancients but superstitious and poetic savages. For their methods of approaching the problems of life were as logical as in our own epoch. After all, why should it not be possible to harmonise all the apparently contradictory conceptions of life and of the universe; by that I mean, probably many of the ancient and many of the modern ideas may be correct. The fantastic theory may be perfectly scientific upon its own plane of manifestation. The yogi or occultist by possessing a knowledge of these unknown laws can produce upon the Earth phenomena, which, not being understood by science, are considered trickery. It is unfortunate for our minds that today we refuse to accept certain phenomena, simply because we have trained our minds to think in a dogmatic way. For instance, because the scientists can imitate the phenomena of Spiritualism, does that prove that Spiritualism is untrue? While the simple fact is that other scientific laws are in operation of which the materialistic scientist is unaware, simply because he has not troubled to give the matter serious investigation. I presume when in some centuries to come only synthetic substances will be made, many of our natural substances that we use nowadays will be thought never to have existed, until science had discovered the way to produce them.

But to return to M.'s teachings regarding the hierarchal forces:

Altogether there are twelve great globes of consciousness, and each globe has its own individual symbol, and it is only by the proper use and understanding of a symbol that the student can contact these globes of consciousness and make known to self the knowledge of their manifestation. For within man there are locked chambers in which is stored the wisdom

gained while passing through these so-called past
cycles; and by the proper use of these symbols the
seeker can unlock to self a knowledge of past endeavours.

M. told me that often he used to sit down and go into
these past periods and come in touch with the Ākāshic
records (a term used by the Theosophists when speaking
about the memory of the Earth); and there he would
see, almost as clearly as one would see an animated picture of three dimensions, the happenings of thousands
of years ago. "The Earth," he said, "has held populations
as dense, and much more so, as in our own time." He
had seen armies upon armies, in countless numbers,
marching and fighting against one another; millions
upon millions, with all their numerous weapons of war
carried in cars. "Man has no conception of what these
great armies had," he continued.

One of the greatest secrets that God can reveal to man
is the knowledge and use of a symbol, for each symbol
has its higher counterpart. As Pythagoras has said:
"As above, so below"; but a selfish man cannot gain
a knowledge of this higher counterpart until Nature
has revealed to him a consciousness of Her reality.
He who would use these sacred mysteries must have
a knowledge of his place and position in Nature; i.e.,
this is his first illumination. For true illumination is
the God within revealing His true nature to the mind
and being of His seeker, and giving a knowledge to
the seeker of his place and position in Nature, which
is really a knowledge of the seeker's own limitations in
this incarnation; giving him an understanding not to

use powers that have no direct bearing upon his present work in life. Man is only happy when he carries out the desires and dictates of his Higher Self. If he does not do so, he generally meets with much opposition and pain, for he must obey that being within himself, who has planned to work in harmony with the laws of God [M. concluded].

I think the reason why we suffer so much is because we have forgotten our divine tasks, whether they be humble or great. Though, as I mention elsewhere, we have to conquer the opposing forces of evil that are sent to us in order to give us strength and experience. If only man discovered his own work in life he would not interfere in the work or beliefs of his fellow-beings. I mention beliefs because I am reminded of the great knowledge possessed by those races holding to religions other than Christianity, and whom we endeavour to convert to beliefs that some of these peoples have long since passed. In our vanity we imagine that truth has been given only to those who call themselves Christians, when great and even more highly developed truths have been given to certain races whom we consider, in the light or darkness of our mechanical civilisation, as uncivilised. Many religious truths have been given by the unseen powers; and according to the mentalities of the people so were the truths adjusted. How pitiful it seems, to see the missionary speak to one who, in culture and breeding, in power and breadth of vision and knowledge, may be immeasurably his superior. If these people who strive to convert the heathen endeavour to discover their own inner powers and work in life, they would help the world in a much finer and nobler manner. By living his own life he would become, as Socrates said, "a midwife who assists souls to birth" (see Plato, *Theaetetus* 150 b–d).

Many of our great social-occult societies become familiar with symbols, but seldom understand their use. Here I will relate an experience I had one evening with M. He wanted me to come with him on a mental trip to Arabia. I did so, and he called my attention to a distinguished looking Arab seated on horseback. I noticed on his wrist a bird, which at first sight I thought was an eagle. But M. told me that it was a falcon; and this was the Arab's messenger to M., who told me that the Arab was known to the brotherhood by his deep and powerful laughter. I mention this incident because M. told me that the Arab could communicate with him, no matter how busily engaged he was. I was also told that this bird was an elemental falcon.

To return to the hierarchal forces again:

These forces that play upon mankind in order to develop and stimulate certain mental and creative properties, though withdrawn for a time, leave behind them a symbol representing each force so that the occultist knows what wisdom cycle governed man at a certain period.

Thus the eternal pageant of divine splendour—whereof our seers have seen but a pale glimmer and have heard but a frailer music, and which has inspired them to mould from these dim echoes an immortal beauty and message for humanity—still lives on. And if one reads the literature of many mystics, and poets, it will be interesting to observe that they often speak of gods and spirits of such a nature that we accept them as being but the wild imaginings of unbalanced minds. Yet the existence of these fantastic and terrible beings is simple to explain from the occult standpoint: that thought is of an eternal nature.

When questioning M. about these gods he told me how they came into being:

> Those civilisations that created in the past certain symbols gave to them a certain mental form as well, which became vital through the collective mind-force of a nation. These mental images were imbued with power and movement; and as man invents machines to work for him, so did these gods do likewise for the ancients. Also, as the people of these past civilisations were very sensitive, they could feel the power of these great presences that they had created. Also these gods, being the fixed forms of the elements, could bring to pass certain phenomena in nature.

As thought never dies, though it may be asleep in the mind, so do I believe these gods are sleeping in this age; but, not believing in them, we do not call upon them, just as we do not call, from the subconscious mind, our old thoughts. Still, I believe they are active enough upon their own plane of manifestation, the plane about which I write in the next chapter. Incidentally, I may mention, one of M.'s pupils told me that she saw the sphere of intelligences from which William Blake drew his pictures.

But in my first mental flight I saw little of these places and gods, though later on, as I developed my mental sight to the intensely higher and more subtle vibrations,

I saw many strange elementals. Yet how difficult it is to write about places that the white races of today consider to be impossible fantasies.

To continue about these gods created by man: I was told that often a great and noble ideal called forth from many minds creates a god of elemental nature. Therefore, despite man's denial of their existence, he still creates his gods and devils. And the astral, so much studied by the Spiritualist and the Theosophist, is but the result of man's disordered imagination. Therefore, man being the subject of his own mental and emotional environment he becomes likewise enslaved to them.

There are many people who are sensitive to other vibrations of consciousness which ordinary people cannot conceive or understand, and many of them suffer from this sensitivity and are apt to be trodden upon by those more blatant and more coarsely fibred. These people are often more wise than their taskmasters, for brute force is seldom sensitive and can generally be touched only through the heart. An instance of sensitivity can be mentioned in regard to the Irish. They are a people who have been subjected to a vibration which is seldom found in other countries; and when they emigrate, they disturb by their singular mental vitality the more placid and conservative minds, awakening them to a greater mental activity. There are also places on the Earth that can be likened to the cup of the spirit [M. concluded].

THE SILVER SILENCE

Here in this silver silence, beyond the dark marge of the present, we dwell and dream; here are serene woods, deer-haunted, where birds too delicate for Earth weave their light arias in the gentle songs of running waters; here are lofty hills, range beyond range, stretching into ever clearer heights without end, yet so smooth that the tender feet of children find them easy to walk upon. And the dwellers beyond those hills are so pure that they are as wisps of flame, for they are the wise children of God, and their words of love and guidance flow down upon the fresh beauty of the wind. Here are moss-mantled glades, where temples, simple and old, shaped like giant flowers, stand ever open to the silver light shining from the plumes of the eternal morning. Come, brothers of the dusk, into the open spaces where the soft bloom of eternity rests on all.

Here the god in you, the divine imagination, will awaken, and the red robes of desire be cast off and burnt. No more will the wild maelstrom of the years gather you into its icy fierceness. Come; leave the academies and universities that seek nourishment from old plants! Has their knowledge opened the gates of the spirit? Lovely was the old, but still more lovely shall be the new. For here beyond the roof of Time are new compasses and new ways of measuring.

Here in the peace we await you.

CHAPTER FOUR

TRAVELS ON THE MENTAL PLANES

For over two years I practiced the various exercises given me by M., in which period I awakened my sleeping clairvoyant faculties and developed them slowly and surely. I never knew I possessed this power until after many meetings with M., when he suggested to me one evening whether I would care to see for him. And I found that I could do so, to my great surprise; for though I had seen in vision many beautiful things, I had never had the power to awaken this gift. It would come to me suddenly, when least expected, but under M.'s tuition I could evoke it whenever I pleased, though the results were not always satisfactory; the atmosphere of a city and country influencing this gift of second sight.

In respect to this power it is interesting to note that, if one is in the company of people who possess certain gifts, this companionship develops similar qualities in oneself, though it is obvious that the person must be sensitive. For mental environment produces a similar effect to physical environment.

And after these two years of constant training M. told me that soon I would be given the interesting experience of journeying out of the body into the mental world. This experience I looked forward to with great eagerness, for he had often spoken to me about his adventures upon the other planes, though it should be noted that I only speak about the mental realms. There are many other planes to the occultist; but as this book is dealing only with the mental aspect of things, little mention will be made about those other places.

I am fully aware that to modern science these things sound absurd and impossible. But as the scientist has been compelled to revise many of his past conceptions, so, I think, will he be compelled in the light of new knowledge to admit many apparently fantastic theories as commonplace and simple facts. And personally my experiences in Spiritualism force me to accept the existence of another discarnate consciousness that exists without this envelope of flesh; a consciousness complete with senses, form and knowledge, moving in its subtler atmosphere with perfect awareness of its being away from the physical body. For I recollect certain experiences when my body lay asleep, in which I travelled in full consciousness, with a knowledge that my body lay slumbering and that I was voyaging in another sphere; one incident particularly impressing me, for I felt that I had left my body permanently, and I kept saying: "But this is frightful; I must return as I have not yet completed my work." I may state that my realisations of an inner existence were as complete as any realisation of earth-consciousness; also I know that my body was far away and asleep. I have met many others who have had similar experiences, though I can hear the amateur and professional psychoanalyst saying: "Oh I can explain that. So simple. It was a wish fulfilment." I leave them to their explanation, which means nothing in this particular case, other than that they had never had such an experience or had disregarded it as insufficient proof of a discarnate consciousness.

To the Theosophists this chapter should be of interest as their literature has generally dealt with a form of astral consciousness inasmuch as they have taken little interest in the planes above the astral; though I believe extremely little, if any, information has been given regarding these higher and less illusive realms.

M. told me, in answer to my questions regarding

these mental realms, that such a form of consciousness and travelling was like stepping from a narrow and dark prison-cell into wider and purer spaces, where one can see cities and peoples, seas and mountains and many wonderful temples about which our world knows little. He mentioned once that he had seen a city of about fifteen million people, the city's architecture being colourful and very beautiful, and the people very wise and ruled over by a great spiritual being.

When I think of the worlds into which M. travels, I can understand why he is so patient in accepting all the small and intolerable burdens of life, for to him this plane is so small that it would be unworthy in the light of a greater knowledge to note the pettiness of people. In all his teachings this world plays its important part in the development of humanity's soulgrowth. But when one has the power to step from the body as though from a door, can one possess still the same narrowness of vision and understanding that the other prisoners hold?

M. told me that, in stepping out of the body, the senses are much more alert, much more so than on this plane, and that the method of locomotion is flight; but of that I shall speak later. In these subtle realms, he told me, dwell the gods man has imagined to be mythical. And when I told him that I had seen in some of my past visions buildings whose designs were so superb and vital that they irradiated an atmosphere as though they possessed a conscious existence, he mentioned that he had seen things of a similar nature, so beautiful that he remembered one incident in which a pupil refused to travel further but clapped her hands like a child. He also spoke about immense mountain peaks upon which were perched cities of great splendour that possessed a royal serenity, while tiers of bridges many miles long stretched towards other cities perched upon similar heights.

It was in the evening when I first visited M., ready and eager to learn about the mental plane. But before I continue I will relate one incident in order that a little proof of the reality of such things may be known. This occurred with M. and myself; yet though it did not deal with the mental planes it did demonstrate to me about another form of travelling out of the body, there being, I understand, many other methods.

A mutual friend of ours, who was likewise a student of the ancient science, travelled a few years ago to Africa; and, not having heard from him for a considerable time, we were anxious about his welfare. So one evening M. asked me if I would like to accompany him upon a mental flight to Africa, to which invitation obviously I assented. Leaving our bodies in the usual manner, we rapidly discovered in what place our friend dwelt. It happened to be in a small hut in a jungle. A few miles away we saw a campfire and, seated nearby, a witch-doctor with two natives, one being the witch-doctor's pupil and wearing a bowler hat. M. told me laughingly that they were smoking a vile kind of tobacco. I have not yet developed a complete consciousness in regard to these mental senses on these trips, but I understand that as one practices, so do these senses awaken. This witch doctor possessed a certain thing that we wished him to give to our friend, and it was for that reason that we visited him. Later we returned to our friend, who lay asleep, and soon after returned to our bodies. A few days later M. wrote to our distant friend and stated our attempts to get in touch with him, and M. also gave him a description of the witch-doctor and mentioned the pupil wearing a bowler hat. Some months later we received a reply in which our friend stated that all was exactly as described, and that he had attempted to get friendly with the witch-doctor, but with little success so far. What other explanation the scientist may have to prove that this was not an occult experience I should be pleased to hear.

To return now to my first mental journey, though travelling was vague it must not be imagined that I lay in a trance, for this was not so. On the contrary, my senses were more acute and sensitive to the slightest sound in the room and in the street than ever before, and M.'s voice sounded louder, though he told me afterwards that he was speaking in quite low tones. In this experience no attempt was made to lull the senses.

Furthermore, if the reader imagines that much that I saw was the result of hypnosis, I think I can prove the contrary, for there were many things M. noticed when I travelled with him I could not see, despite my attempts to do so. Also I saw things that M. did not see. Therefore I think my conclusions are correct, for had I been merely a subject I should have seen anything that M. desired. There were some things I wished most eagerly to see but I could not.

Afterwards M. told me that one developed a form of twin consciousness, in which one dwelt in the mental realms and moved about in an atmosphere that was most pleasing to the occultist. In a later journey he showed me his home on the higher realms. It was of an earlier period and he was dressed in a different costume; also his features were different. The reason for this change in dress and time was, he told me, that the soul loves to dwell in the age that had given it the greatest happiness, and in which it had been able to do the greatest good.

Therefore, contradictory as it may seem, the fully developed occultist can dwell in two places at once; to give an example, if we could be conscious of the working of our subconscious mind at the same moment when we were doing something else, we might have a somewhat feeble conception of this form of twin consciousness.

Above all things, M. told me, the most difficult in the early mental travels is locomotion, and I found it to be so. It was most difficult to travel upwards and onwards, and only through M.'s prompting and guidance was I enabled to climb, though I never saw M., as he was behind watching and helping me. I could not levitate because I had in the first place to contest against the darker forces of past conditions that attempted to pull me down. For one who endeavours to enter his own true plane of being and Nature is faced by two forces: firstly, the white representing the present and the future; and secondly, the darker forces representing the past, which attempt to drag the adventuring spirit into lower conditions. M. also told me that in order to develop perfect consciousness in these higher realms one must conquer three schools of magicians: the dark magicians of the Earth, for magicians dwell upon this plane; the astral-plane magicians who use the Earth magicians as their instruments—these magicians produce phenomena of a most amazing nature; and thirdly, the mental magicians who use the astral magicians also as their instruments. One must conquer these three forces, representing the masters of magic; one power that is incarnated upon this planet and the other two upon the astral and the mental.

Therefore, the reason why we have to start from

the higher places, about which I shall speak later, is in order to avoid the Earthbound and astral conditions if possible. I might incidentally mention that M. suggested in cases of spirit obsession, a good cure might be to take the obsessed person to a high mountaintop, as the controlling entity could not ascend into a pure atmosphere and would therefore be driven out. These darker forces that I met strove to keep me within their own sphere, and it was only by constantly concentrating and aspiring to the highest within me, and purifying my mind, that I managed to avoid falling down and being drawn into the darker conditions of the past. Nevertheless, when I had succeeded, later on I had to descend into past periods in order to awaken and release some of my own conditions that still weighed me down, and in that manner as though jumping from a springboard, I rose higher. I might also mention that a few months after this occult experience I saw an ancient Oriental picture, painted in the twelfth century, depicting in symbols the different stages of consciousness, some through which I had passed, and a scene similar to the journey I took with M. It was drawn, I understood, by an initiate monk.

In my later travels I was interested to note that my mental body was considerably different from my physical; and I was told that as one goes further and higher one grows younger, an instance of which I shall mention later.

That evening, with M.'s aid I ascended many mountain ranges. It is interesting to note that in many sacred books mountains are mentioned, and though we may give them spiritual and symbolic interpretations, which probably will be quite correct, for sacred symbols have many meanings and interpretations, yet some may also be taken literally. I also visited certain buildings and only rested when I came to a small and curiously designed halfway-house, wherein I entered; and I remember a feeling of great peace steal over me. Then, rising, I peered from a small window and saw at an immense distance a grey mist; and M. told me that that dark shroud was the Earth. How small it appeared! How melancholy! But that night I felt tired and could travel no further and so returned to the consciousness of my body, wondering whether I had dreamt the incidents of the voyage or whether I had really visited these strange places.

My first journey was the prelude to many more, wherein my mental sight became clearer and wherein I saw many strange things and met people as real as myself. But above all, I noticed, was the love and gentleness sent out from them, particularly those who had developed a Chinese consciousness. For each nation has its spiritual counterpart, even when these nations apparently have vanished from the Earth. And I met the Roman, the Egyptian, and a number of others, each possessing a certain quality; but the Chinese particularly possessed a childlike and gentle atmosphere, though behind this simplicity dwelt a great wisdom and a sense of beauty that loved the refined and the delicate. M. told me that he had seen the very spiritual Chinamen of these realms look like wisps of mist responding to the Rhythm and Pulse of Eternity; and though we Westerners may smile at these so-called heathens who worship their ancestors, I can now understand that they possess much reason and logic in doing so, for they worship the spiritual aspects of man; and those who have travelled further into these higher realms, and accordingly have learned more of spiritual things, possess the power to help those on the Earth who are related to them by blood and love. Now I have learnt that each nation has been given the most suitable aspect of religion. For to the student all religions are true, being but the immortal principles of divine knowledge and law. And I believe religions came to birth to make man ultimately the essence of these spiritual laws. I think if one investigates the various religions that man has followed, it will be noticed that each one contains a special quality not possessed by the others, though each one has for its foundation Love. Therefore the occult student can enter any place of worship, the Church or the Synagogue, the Mosque or the Pagoda. He can visit Mecca and he can indulge wholeheartedly in Chinese ancestor-worship with the same fervour as the native born to it, for he can understand the significance of them all. To quote from Macrobius's *Commentary on "Scipio's Dream"* regarding the reason for dissension among men about divinity:

As soon, therefore, as the soul gravitates towards the body in the first production of herself she begins to experience a material tumult; that is, matter flowing into her essence. And this is what Plato remarks in the *Phaedo* (§ 79c), that the soul is drawn into the body staggering with recent intoxication; signifying by this the new drink of matter's impetuous flood, through which the soul, becoming defiled and heavy, is drawn into a terrene situation . . . . Hence oblivion, the companion of intoxication, there begins silently to creep into the recesses of the soul. FOR IF SOULS RETAINED IN THEIR DESCENT TO BODIES THE MEMORY OF DIVINE CONCERNS, OF WHICH THEY WERE CONSCIOUS IN THEIR HEAVENS, THERE WOULD BE NO

DISSENSION AMONG MEN ABOUT DIVINITY. But all indeed, in descending, drink of oblivion; though some more and others less. On this account, though truth is not apparent to all men on the Earth, yet all exercise their opinions about it; because A DEFECT OF MEMORY IS THE ORIGIN OF OPINION. But those discover most who have drank least of oblivion, because they easily remember what they have known before in the Heavens. (ch. 12, §§ 7–10)

Thus the occult student who delves more deeply into the inner meanings of religion can understand and sympathise with those apparently contradictory beliefs, found in nearly every country of the world. As M. says, "Each religion is but a page of a still greater book"; and from the savage who worships his small idol to the mystic who worships the whole universe—all read the truths of God according to the intelligence given to them by Him. And I venture to say that not one of them are wrong until the poison of fanaticism makes them run amok and attack those who worship other gods. And herein lies the importance of an occult training, for the student knowing and realising the different and hidden laws that command humanity brings to all things a different and more *tolerant* valuation, though his toleration would not extend to the destructive agents. His eyes have a different way of looking at things, for he has entered into a more philosophic world, wherein he does not stand in judgment against men, so much as he attempts to discern those hidden motives that make men do things that may harm or help them. For the occultist has also been a psychoanalyst, and has been so for ages. He can follow and unravel the tangled thoughts beyond the regions of the mind, and where the modern psychoanalyst leaves off, he continues; for he can function consciously upon the mental plane or the world of mind where thought-action is as real to him as physical emotion is to those moving about on this planet. He can examine upon the mental body the diseased spots of the mind as easily as the doctor the diseases of the physical body.

But not alone is the occultist a student of religion, for his interests lie in all things, though as I mention elsewhere he is generally a specialist in one particular aspect of life. He is as greatly interested in the latest scientific discovery as the scientist would be, in the development of a political situation, or in the latest phase of art, for he is one to whom all knowledge and world events fit in as harmoniously and as perfectly as in a piece of cabinet work. He must be prepared to move in all forms of society and listen to babes and sages with an open heart, for he knows that all men are instruments used by the gods, and truths may be unconsciously delivered to him through them.

The impressions I felt after my mental voyages were of my own extreme littleness, the smallness and darkness of the Earth, and a new understanding in regard to the unseen forces of evil that move upon these subtler planes; and also the powers that use the artist, the poet and the prophet, inspiring them and giving them new conceptions and emotions.

Does the genius who receives his inspiration from these hidden powers, if conscious that he is being used, ever acknowledge his indebtedness to the unseen helpers? How many creators know where their ideas come from; who gives to them the poem, the melody, the picture that shakes the world? As I have already written of the manner in which knowledge is drawn from the higher planes, I shall but refer the reader to those beliefs I hold.

It is also noticeable that much of our creative works have distinct traces of old civilisations, and some have characteristics of periods unknown to us. I think the possible explanation from the occultist's standpoint is that these great minds had contacted the past and possible future periods of these mental realms; though of course it is understood that I am speaking of art which inspires man and holds a message for him, not a mechanical process of uninspired technique, a form of mental craftsmanship that by sheer weight of mass has attempted to overthrow the pantheon of Beauty. But to continue! Possibly this may explain why these creators of a strange form of beauty were not understood until after many years, until the unseen forces sent to this world new influences into the many minds of its dwellers; and only then were they comprehended and acceptable who in previous years were despised.

Many of our critics attempt to enslave time, striving to keep the future years with their messages at bay. But despite the outbursts against that which holds a new principle of beauty, these new forms like small seeds grow irresistibly and slowly into the minds of the younger generation, and also ultimately become the commonplace and obviously understood; these often unconscious messengers of the gods having fulfilled their mission leave this world, returning to those realms that are to us still the future.

M. has told me to think of the present and the future, but never of the past.

Place the mind only in the present and the future, for the past wills us to become its object. The future brings its mystery to light in the mind of the seeker and nothing ever happens to the student of occultism until he has passed into the mind-atmosphere of the inner worlds of being, for to deal only with objective things is only to produce objective conditions. The power to pass into these inner states is not very easy unless one has been trained in the school of the most developed mental Adepts or Masters. To ascend to the planes of these mental worlds we must bury the past conditions and levitate our minds to the highest possible spheres. The average student lacks discipline, and few have patience to develop this power. I can only show you the way out of the body, but we must succeed in the lesser practices before the Will can strengthen itself in order to make the mind its servant. Though if you wish to be taken to any part of this world in the occult manner it is not very difficult.

I have already described such an instance in the beginning of this chapter.

Though I speak of art in regard to the higher planes, it should be remembered that the darker forces that strove to prevent my ascending also influence many who create, and often they produce that unhealthy design and form which evokes a stream of unclean passion. These are forces that flow from the astral and the mental hells, though fortunately M. did not take me to these places. Yet I understood that when one has grown sufficiently strong, one is also brought before these evil elements in order to know the causes that produce sufferings and obsessions in humanity. M. calls them for want of a better term "the Luciferians"; and he told me of a particular instance when he saw the evil in one of them dying. It lay in a crystal coffin and it gazed at him with eyes that held a strange and terrible wisdom. Evil had been its nature. Its body was beautiful and harmonious in proportion, but of a form inconceivable to man. I have also seen a group of evil beings, and the impressions I received all seemed to dwell in their eyes, which sent out a great magnetic and malignant glare, filled with a great power. I told of my vision to M., and mentioned a curious feature about their heads, and he told me it was a symbol showing that they possessed great knowledge.

In one trip a most remarkable thing was shown me, something extremely difficult to believe, yet from the occult aspect quite easily understood. It is known to occultists and Theosophists that many of the things we do on this plane have been preordained, the work that we do in art or in anything else has already been accomplished upon these higher planes. I have seen inventions mentally that materialised afterwards upon this Earth. These things have been accomplished usually by our Higher Selves; and that may explain the problem of clairvoyance, for what has been created on these planes is still in the period we would call the future, and the sensitive clairvoyant who has opened the inner eye can see into these realms; though the ordinary medium sees things often in the astral, which we consider to be the realm of illusion.

One evening M. took me upon a mental trip, wherein I travelled with great difficulty. Something seemed to pull me downward and it was only with M.'s help that I managed to arrive at the place he desired to show me. It was a small room in which a young child was writing, while through a nearby window a great shaft of silver light came flowing. I looked at the child and seemed to recognise him as somebody I had known long ago. I asked M. if he could tell me who the child was and heard with astonishment that it was myself upon this mental plane. I have mentioned previously that as one goes further one appears younger, for I had seen myself as a youth of about fourteen. I also know another case of a pupil who was like a little girl, and M. himself has told me that when he approached these higher and purer realms he also became as a child, and the saying that only a child can see God is literally true upon this higher plane. For a child is impersonal and, therefore, sees more clearly. To continue my own experience, another curious thing I noticed was that as the child gazed up into the stream of light, the face grew younger; but when he bent down, the face grew very old. M. told me I was writing a book that would appear in the future, which did not surprise me, for I had often seen complete new poems in my dreams; for in sleep the soul journeys to its realm of true being, with clear metrical forms and subjects, which were ultimately written, though many were also unwritten, as I could not recollect the words. I believe many writers have had such an experience. M. also told me that the reason why we found it so difficult to travel this time was because two magicians wished to prevent my journeying to this realm. For when we awaken the finer part of ourselves we also stir the lower aspects of our character, as all occult students know, which immediately sends out a challenge to do battle with our higher qualities, and that is what occurred in this instance. M. also told me that our past lives are sometimes like weights that hold and pull the body down to past periods; and, as I mentioned elsewhere, we have to descend into these darker regions in order to snap the links that would prevent us from aspiring; also we view the deeds wrought in those past lives in order to understand the motives that guided them, and such an experience teaches us to be more careful in our thoughts and actions; also, when we have undergone such an occult experience, we can understand the things of this world much more clearly. In regard to that aspect I think a few pages dealing with the mental powers used today upon mankind will not be out of place.

One of the most terrible powers used upon mankind is hypnotism; terrible because it is unseen and often used by unscrupulous people whose victims are seldom conscious of this danger working upon them.

There are many phases of this force, of which the least is self-suggestion; and the greatest, crowd hypnosis, whereby a whole nation can be plunged into a whirlpool of passion and hate, driving them to destruction; a force that unbalances millions of people, obsessing them until a certain object has been attained. Man is not master of this planet. He may hold power for a time over certain elements, and in so doing pride himself upon his strength until the terrible moment comes when a titanic catastrophe overwhelms him. Boastful cities become curtained in golden veils of flame; the ground of the Earth trembles and undulates like the waves of an ocean, while here and there her mouths gape widely and swallow and lick with her tongues of flame man and his works; and inasmuch as he is not master of this planet materially, neither is he master of his mind, nor of his emotions. Many of his thoughts and feelings are not his own; he may enter a crowd and emerge with a strange desire or a strange thought that is totally alien to his character. A slight instance can be mentioned as proof, showing that in these minute incidents lie hidden the unknown laws. One evening David and myself attended a meeting at the Theosophical

Society, and while we were listening strange thoughts came into my mind. I turned to David and noticed that he was likewise puzzled. Suddenly, without my asking him, he turned and said, "Mr. X—— is here"; and we both understood immediately. The number of people who have had such experiences is probably past counting, and how many have been unconsciously used by other people is likewise. We take too little heed of such instances, yet I believe that witchcraft and magic certainly exist today, but have a different terminology; and these powers are of far too subtle a nature for science to experiment with, even if it accepted the existence of such things. Imagine a person who has developed telepathy to its highest degree, who can send his thoughts to whomsoever he desires and make that person obey him. Would that not be a clear case of hypnosis and a form of obsession which modern science ignores? People may commit crimes when they are temporarily obsessed, and when they have accomplished their purpose they become sane again; but that person who is but an instrument is either imprisoned or hanged, while the real criminal may be far away. True it is difficult to discover whether the criminal was guilty or not, but nevertheless the possibilities of crimes being committed by people far away from the scene remains.

Another aspect of the same power is in the many modern business-schools where the training is openly hypnosis. "Weaken the mind of your client. It does not matter whether he wants your goods or not; force him to buy. Discover his weakness and plunge like a lance all your mental force into those feeble parts and he is bound to succumb." It is as though one used a mental club. If one used a stone club, one would be imprisoned, and rightly so. But unfortunately for the victim one uses an unseen club. It is difficult to detain such a mental savage and place him in a spot wherein he could do the least harm. Yet this form of training flourishes today all over the world. And because it is too subtle a form of brigandage we have to permit it to exist, though it is unfortunate that society cannot frame a new form of jurisprudence to deal solely with mental criminals, for they are a much greater danger than the normal ones.

Here I shall quote a few notes upon the preceding subject given to me by M.

Great is the mind that can leave every other mind alone. One has no right to use one's powers in order to inquire into the affairs of others unless asked to do so by that person, for the soul does not wish the great law to be broken. The advanced student must only speak of the things that the Higher Self of the questioner wishes its personality to know, and the student must contact his own Higher Self before he can contact the Higher Self of the questioner. If the student gives information and knowledge which limits the freedom of expression of the other soul, *he must be prepared to bear the Karma of the questioner*. In regard to the mental criminals, there are laws governing the mental planes as well as the physical, and the criminal will also be punished by imprisoning himself when he passes over.

The main use of clairvoyance is to distinguish that stage of soul-evolution that the soul had reached, for what is called "right knowledge of the Greater Mysteries" is never given to a soul that has not developed the power of the right use of knowledge. It is said, "By a man's light is he known"; and every soul answers the proper challenge given by the teacher, and through clairvoyance the teacher knows whether the student may be given the right instruction. Clairvoyance is a physical acquirement; just as man develops his body, so with correct teachings he may develop clairvoyance, and regarding this power of true clairvoyance one must reach a stage of development in order to understand the laws that govern its uses. Otherwise the light which gives him clear seeing will be taken away, for the soul will not permit its gifts to be illegitimately used. Nature places a wonderful book before man; and if he will but open his eyes, he will be able to read many unbelievable things about which he knows little nowadays, for he can extend his consciousness through many realms and become familiar with Her teachings, for God is never apart from His creations.

Then M. continued further in answer to some questions in regard to the mental body:

You ask me for some rule that may destroy ignorance in your mental body. A child seeks to know all about the world in which it has been born; so seek to find from your own true instructor, the Mind of your Master who dwells within your own true world of being, the way to your own inner wisdom. You can follow Him by your instinctive sense, and by doing so find that your own inner world can be made more real to your lower understanding. You have been taken to the realms of the mental body, and in those trips sensed the relationship between the outer and inner selves. Do not forget this, for these spheres to which I have taken you correspond to the inner planes of being.

You found yourself aged on the world plane, but you found that age disappears as you pass onwards to the realities of being. You came to a place where you were able to see yourself as a boy, and you found that your mind had become very quick and alert, with an understanding of things which you do not possess on this plane. And you felt that within your atmosphere great powers were at work that endeavoured to give you an atmosphere of their own nature. You can build this mental atmosphere into your prose and poems.

I took you to your workshop on an inner plane, and you could see yourself at work and that Ray of Light from whence you draw force and power. You were also conscious of the two powers that attempted to hold you in their thrall, powers with which you have to contend ere reaching your true destination. But when you were able to contact that Ray of Light, you were able to annul those minds who opposed you. You were writing on that plane the opening sentence of your book, "O Merlin! etc.," and since then we endeavoured to help you to remember what you were writing.

You realise that man is a composite being having different powers of which the objective man knows but little, and it was to teach you the existence of these living inner powers that I took you into the hidden planes, the source of divine realities.

EPILOGUE

Here for a time end those teachings my Master has given me. Whether they will be regarded by the reader as ancient truths reawakened, or but the fantastic beliefs of a student, I do not know. But I do know that many of these things taught to me have brought realisations and greater understanding of those unknown laws of Nature in relation to the ordinary affairs of life. That I have found much difficulty to live according to many of these teachings can be understood; for I have studied but a few years, and it is difficult to smooth the sharp angles and crude corners of character in a little while. I feel that those students and seekers who, like myself, believe that somewhere on this planet dwell mightier brothers, who move nations as we move chess-pieces, will read in much that I have written some new principles that many works dealing with kindred subjects have either neglected or have not known.

That readers of a scientific frame of mind will treat with great scepticism much that I have written, I am fully aware, and from their standpoint, not having studied these things, I can understand them doing so; for they can only look with suspicion upon those who bring forward teachings that demand a moral method of investigation instead of a chemical method. Though I think I may state that I stand upon as firm a ground in my investigations as many scientists have done in the past, for have they not dogmatically asserted the truths of their theories, which later on were found to be incorrect? Whether these teachings are found to be likewise can only be judged after being attempted, which I leave to future occult investigators.

*   *   *   *   *

Incarnation after incarnation have we erected noble civilisations to our far-soaring dreams; we have heard the music of their swift wings in the calm ancient evenings of our past births, when we wondered whether the stars were the silver nests of the winged ones. We have sailed unknown seas and have disembarked upon sands that man's feet have never pressed; we have listened to the lisping cadences of leaf and the small melody of bird, thinking that our dreams were bewitched and imprisoned in the song of Nature; upon coloured isles where Lotus-eaters lay swooning, their melting senses enchanted by too much richness, have we trod and sought in the jewelled glens for the immortal Truths; we have left our cloaks of clay in every land, upon every mountain crest, enriching the dust of the world and melting away in the waters, while the restless flame of the soul journeyed on in travail, still seeking its lost divinity; still striving to hear the symphony of its own inner God, that chord that would lift it up and make it one with its own small universe.

Have we not felt when our moods rise above the trammels of flesh the hallowed and cool flame of the indwelling God bathing our souls, and ascending with us in smooth and unhurried manner to the calm heights of the spirit, where the loftier remembrance of an immortal existence unfolded itself like a perfect flower. For a moment the passions that anchor us to Earth are loosened, and the dark desires of life are erased, and upon the palimpsest are inscribed the eternal words of Truth to illuminate our hearts when we again descend, bringing us for a little while a quiet joy that vanishes too soon when we become thralls again to our sorrows and lower moods. And it is only when we can train ourselves to voyage to the altar of contemplation whensoever we please that we can develop a perpetual consciousness of those higher altitudes, and from those shining eyries, see the ocean of gold that envelops the whole globe and humanity, making us one. And it is in order that man rediscovers those lost regions and his ancient heritage, his own inner treasure-house, that this work has been written. For through the ages those brothers who have found peace call also to others to seek the sovereign balm.

THE AWAKENING

Soon the heavy and sluggish forms of the dark and sightless centuries, who have hooded with their bat-like cloaks the eyes of man, shall be dispersed by the courier winds of the returning gods. For man has wooed and knelt too long before the bloodless phantoms of decay; the spent glamour of age can hold no nourishment for the flowering of aspiration, and therefore the gods return to bring new melody, new art and new understanding. Through the billowing and sun-enbraided wings of Earth that border the azure and infinite horizon shines dimly for the moment a growing splendour; then suddenly the cloudy pinions crumble, and there rises in marshalled regality the swift, silver-bridled horses, harnessed to glowing chariots wherein stand the youthful and virgin gods, golden-helmed and greaved, whose glinting armour is undinted and untarnished. They are the celestial dynasties and ethereal children born from the divine and eternal mother, Flame, whose breasts are the stars that have suckled these children upon a fiery milk. Soon shall we hear the shrill neighing of the horses and the tempests choiring amid their tossing manes. The rolling chariots leave a wake of light within the air as they plunge upon the white-crested parapets of mountain peak. While the thunders from the gods, unleashed, shall be the resurgam of truths singing like triumphant trumpets, once again awakened as they burst through the hooded centuries to free imprisoned minds.

*   *   *   *   *

Sweet is the birth
Of sweeter Earth;
Clear, calm and cool the skies.
For greater powers
Send forth their flowers
Whose perfume purifies.
The soul of man
Moves to a plan,
Guided by God and gods,
Who lead aright
Each weary knight
From darker periods.
Immutable,
Inscrutable,
Were all the roads of old.
Now every sign
Is crystalline,
And every path is gold.

BIBLIOGRAPHY

The following list of works is intended to help the reader interested in following up on a particular passage or exploring more thoroughly the works of those authors cited in the main text. It is not suggested that these are the exact editions used by Juste.

A.E. [George William Russell]. *The Candle of Vision*. London: Macmillan, 1918.

Blake, William. "Auguries of Innocence." In *The Complete Poetry and Prose of William Blake*, revised ed., edited by David V. Erdman, pp. 490–93. Berkeley and Los Angeles: University of California Press, 1982.

Blavatsky, H. P. *The Secret Doctrine: The Synthesis of Science, Religion, and Philosophy*. 2 vols. London: Theosophical Publishing Company, 1888. [Reprinted in photographic facsimile, Pasadena, California: Theosophical University Press, 1999.]

Paracelsus. *The Hermetic and Alchemical Writings of Aureolus Philippus Theophrastus Bombast, of Hohenheim, Called Paracelsus the Great: Now for the First Time Faithfully Translated into English; Edited with a Biographical Preface, Elucidatory Notes, a Copious Hermetic Vocabulary, and Index by Arthur Edward Waite*. 2 vols. London: James Ellion, 1894.

Pryse, James Morgan. *The Restored New Testament: The Hellenic Fragments Freed from the Pseudo-Jewish Interpolations, Harmonized, and Done into English Verse and Prose; With Introductory Analysis, and Commentaries, Giving an Interpretation According to Ancient Philosophy and Psychology; And a New Literal Translation of the Synoptic Gospels, with Introduction and Commentaries*. Los Angeles: James M. Pryse; London: John Watkins, 1914.

Thompson, Francis. "The Mistress of Vision" In *New Poems*, pp. 3–13. New York: John Lane, 1908.

Villars, Abbé N. de Montfaucon de. *Comte de Gabalis: Rendered out of French and into English with a Commentary*. New York and London: published by the Brothers, 1914.

Wilde, Oscar. *The Picture of Dorian Gray*. London, New York, and Melbourne: Ward Lock, [1891]. [Reprinted countless times by numerous publishers.]

www.ingramcontent.com/pod-product-compliance
Lightning Source LLC
Chambersburg PA
CBHW031510120626
46545CB00005B/1814